God and Timelessness

God and Timelessness

by
NELSON PIKE

Wipf and Stock Publishers
EUGENE, OREGON

Wipf and Stock Publishers
199 West 8th Avenue, Suite 3
Eugene, Oregon 97401

God and Timelessness
By Pike, Nelson
©1970 Pike, Nelson
ISBN: 1-57910-878-4
Publication date: January, 2002
Previously published by Schocken Books, Inc., 1970.

To

John Pike sr.

Contents

	PREFACE	page ix
	INTRODUCTION: TWO WORKING ASSUMPTIONS	1
1.	THE PREDICATE 'TIMELESS'	6
2.	THE LOGICAL STATUS OF 'GOD IS TIMELESS'	17
3.	TIMELESSNESS AND THE NEGATIVE PREDICATES 'IMMUTABLE', 'INCORRUPTIBLE' AND 'IMMORTAL'	39
4.	TIMELESSNESS, FOREKNOWLEDGE AND FREE WILL	53
5.	TIMELESS KNOWLEDGE OF WHAT IS HAPPENING NOW	87
6.	TIMELESSNESS AND POWER	97
7.	GOD AS A TIMELESS PERSON	121
8.	THE JUSTIFICATION OF THE DOCTRINE OF TIMELESSNESS: ANSELM	130
9.	THE JUSTIFICATION OF THE DOCTRINE OF TIMELESSNESS: SCHLEIERMACHER	167
	A CONCLUDING COMMENT	189
	INDEX	191

Preface

Within the technical, theological tradition of the Christian religion there have been suggested at least two ways of understanding the notion of God's eternity. Some theologians have said that God is eternal in that His life is indefinitely extended both forward and backward in time. On this view, to say that God is eternal is to say that the life of God has unending duration. God always has and always will exist. On the other hand, a considerable number of important Christian theologians (both Catholic and Protestant) have held that as applied to God, the term 'eternal' is not to be understood as meaning 'unending duration'. The life of God has no duration – God exists, as they say, 'outside of time'. To say that God is eternal is to say that God is 'timeless'. In this essay, I shall undertake an examination of this second way of understanding the notion of God's eternity. The effort will be to investigate the traditional theological doctrine of timelessness from as many angles as have appeared to me to provide fruitful perspective.

My interest in this project stems from two sources.

First, the position that a theologian takes on the topic of divine eternity has a kind of controlling effect on the general shape and texture of his broad theological view about the nature of God. As I shall try to show in Ch. 3, if a theologian holds that God is timeless (rather than everlasting) he is committed to a very specific interpretation of the negative modal predicates used in theological discourse – predicates such as 'immutable' and 'incorruptible'. Thus, when a theologian says that God is eternal in the sense of timeless, he must stand ready to endorse the implications of this claim as regards these other negative attributes of God. In similar fashion, the interpretation one assigns to the predicate 'eternal' has an important bearing on the doctrine of divine omniscience. Some traditional theologians have thought that if God is everlasting (rather than timeless) the doctrine of divine omniscience entails determinism. On the other hand, some contemporary philosophers have argued that if God is timeless (rather than everlasting) he cannot be omniscient at all. A corresponding set of problems and issues arise with respect to the logical relations between 'eternal' and 'omnipotent' and the logical relations between 'eternal' and 'person'. In short, the predicate 'eternal' occupies something of a pivotal position within the logical-geography of traditional Christian thinking about the nature of God. A good deal rests on how one interprets this predicate when attempting to construct, comprehend or evaluate a theological system. Yet, in spite of the centrality of the doctrine of eternity, theologians and philosophers of religion have not always been clear about the details of its alternative interpretations. In particular, the precise implications of the theological doctrine of timelessness have not been well understood even by many who have included this doctrine in their own theological systems. It was this realization that first prompted my interest in this topic. The presence of conceptual obscurity is an invitation to the philosopher. This is an invitation to which I am responding in undertaking this project.

Secondly, for the past two decades (or more), there has been considerable discontent within the Christian theological community about the picture of God that is presented in the classical theological literature. One object of dissatisfaction has been the traditional insistence on the utter *transcendence* of God. Contemporary theologians influenced by the writings of A. N. Whitehead have complained that a being

Preface

who is transcendent in the way specified within the mainstream of Christian theology is not 'religiously available'. A more outspoken version of this protest has been heard recently from followers of Bishop James Robinson. When considered as a supreme being 'out there' and apart from mundane objects and happenings, God, they have assured us, is dead. Now, if one surveys the range of doctrines that have been advanced in traditional Christian theological texts concerning the nature of God, the claim that God is timeless must surely be listed as the most complete and emphatic assertion of divine transcendence. According to this doctrine, God is not only 'out there' and apart from the world of temporal objects and happenings, God is 'out there' and removed from time altogether. It would thus seem that an explication and evaluation of the doctrine of timelessness might be of considerable help to those of us who are interested in contemporary theological trends. There can be no intelligent appraisal of a protest until there has been a careful investigation of that towards which the protest is directed. Though a look at the doctrine of timelessness cannot be expected to furnish all of the data that will be needed for the final evaluation of contemporary misgivings about the traditional concept of God, the fact that this doctrine is the ultimate expression of God's transcendence suggests that this might be a good place to begin. It is my hope that this study will be of some use to those who will eventually push an investigation of this sort through to completion.

This essay is made up of nine chapters. They can be thought of as grouping into three broad divisions. In the first two chapters, I attempt to clarify the statement 'God is timeless'. My purpose in these opening discussions is to identify the logical status of this statement as it occurs in the theological texts in which it is affirmed. The next five chapters contain studies of the logical connections between the predicate 'timeless' and a number of other predicates normally used in theological texts when describing the

Supreme Being. Here I examine timelessness as it relates to other negative attributes such as immutability and incorruptibility. I also look at the connections between timelessness and a number of positive attributes such as omnipotence and omniscience. In the last two chapters I confront the problem of justifying the doctrine of timelessness using patterns of reasoning usually employed by traditional Christian theologians when supporting claims about the nature of God. Two such justification-procedures are examined. The conclusion in each case is that the doctrine of timelessness does not lend itself to justification under the procedure in question. In a concluding remark at the very end, I suggest that it is extremely hard to understand why the doctrine of timelessness has had a place in traditional Christian theology.

Although the first purpose of each of the chapters included in this volume is to clarify and/or evaluate the doctrine of timelessness, I have also tried to say some things of value on a number of other theological and philosphical topics, e.g., the medieval doctrine of essential predication (Ch. 2), the traditional problem of divine foreknowledge (Ch. 4) and the general methodological issues connected with traditional ways of determining the adequacy of statements ascribing specific attributes to God (Chs. 8 and 9). In some cases, I have developed my ideas on these other topics in more detail than the central concern of the essay would strictly require.

It may not be too much to hope that in addition to any light I may be able to provide with respect to the doctrine of timelessness and the other issues just mentioned, I may also succeed in making some minor contributions to our understanding of several important theological systems; especially those of St. Anselm of Canterbury and Frederich Schleiermacher.

Professor Robert Adams, now at the University of Michigan, and his wife, Mrs. Marilyn Adams, read an early draft of the entire volume. Their comments and

Preface

criticisms were of first importance to me when working out the finished version of this essay. Marilyn Adams's Ph.D. thesis on the topic of divine foreknowledge (unpublished) was the source of several ideas that eventually led to some points made in Chs. 1 and 4. To these two philosophers I am sincerely grateful for the help they gave me when writing this book. Most of all I want to thank each of them individually for providing the kind of stimulation during their years at Cornell that only on outstanding graduate student can give to one who makes his living in the classroom. Their own achievements in philosophy have been, and will continue to be, sources of great satisfaction to me.

There is virtually no chapter in this book that was not made better as a consequence of the searching criticisms and insightful suggestions of Professor John V. Canfield now at the University of Toronto. In particular, Chs. 3, 5 and 8 are free of a number of mistakes and confusions that they originally contained only because of his meticulous philosophical evaluations. I am just one of John Canfield's former colleagues at Cornell who owe him profound thanks for the many times he helped us see the sources of our own philosophical perplexities.

Professor Norman Kretzmann of Cornell University provided an important assist when I was working on the topic of theological predication (Introduction). Norman Kretzmann also checked the English translations of all Latin texts reproduced in the book. Professor Joel Feinberg of Rockefeller University and Professor Norman Malcolm of Cornell University read an early draft of Ch. 2. Norman Malcolm also read an early version of Ch. 8. To these three friends and former colleagues I owe an important debt of gratitude for the hand they so willingly extended in my direction when I was writing this book.

During the summer of 1966 I had many fruitful conversations with Father Norris Clarke S.J. of Fordham University. These conversations helped to crystallize and correct my thinking on a wide range of theological topics – some of which are discussed in this essay. At the other end of the interval during which this book was written, D. Z. Phillips of University College, Swansea, read the whole of what was to be the final version of the text. His comments and suggestions prompted a number of important eleventh-hour changes. I am grateful to both of these men for their respective contributions to my reflections.

The Danforth Foundation supported half of my Sabbatical leave in 1966–7. Had they not provided me with this leisure, I doubt that this book would have been written. I should also like to thank the Humanities Council of Cornell University. It supplied the money to pay the typist. Finally, I am grateful to my wife Carol for the work she did in helping me prepare this book for publication.

Introduction:
Two Working Assumptions

In the course of the deliberations to follow, I assume that God (if He exists) is *a being* – a single individual possessing negative as well as positive attributes. Some contemporary theologians such as, e.g., Paul Tillich and Bishop James Robinson, have urged that God is not to be conceived of as *a* being, i.e., as a single individual bearing qualities. However, that God is *a* being is clearly presupposed by the theologians I shall be discussing in this essay (St. Augustine, Boethius, St. Thomas, St. Anselm, Frederich Schleiermacher and others). I thus make this assumption in order to keep my discussion in line with the basic structure of the theological thinking I shall be examining.

As regards the terms designating the negative attributes usually assigned to God, I discuss their meanings at length in the body of the text. I shall say nothing about them here. However, with respect to positive predicates such as 'perfectly good', 'omnipotent' and 'omniscient', I proceed in a way that might be thought by some to require explanation. I think I had best provide this explanation here rather than later in the discussion where it might escape attention.

Consider the term 'triangle' as it is used in the discourse of geometry. Compare it with 'triangle' as it occurs in the discourse of carpentry or woodworking. Within the discourse of geometry, the criteria governing the use of this term are more strict than are the criteria governing its use in the discourse of carpentry. The geometrical figure is an exemplary (i.e., perfect) version of the shape embodied in the triangular block of wood. We reach an understanding of the geometrical triangle by correcting imperfections (irregularities) in the shape of the triangular block. Now let's ask whether 'triangle' has the same meaning in the two cases. We might answer this question in either way. Once the relation between the criteria governing its use in the two cases is made clear, no one would be confused if we were to say that 'triangle' has the same meaning in the two cases, and no one would be confused if we were to say that 'triangle' has different meanings in the two cases. Regarding the relation between the criteria in question, the following point seems to me to be of considerable importance. If a block of wood is triangular, it has three angles that add up (roughly) to 180 degrees and its sides are (roughly) straight. *At least this much is implied* with respect to the geometrical figure when one characterizes it as a triangle. By this I mean that if one could find reasons sufficient for rejecting the claim that a given thing is a triangle as 'triangle' is used in the discourse of carpentry (suppose that one of its sides is visibly curved, or suppose that it has four angles), these reasons would be sufficient for rejecting the claim that the thing in question is a triangle as 'triangle' is used in the discourse of geometry. In fact, more than this can be said. If one could find slight irregularities in the shape of a thing that would cause hesitation or prompt reservation about whether it was a triangle as 'triangle' is used in the discourse of carpentry, such irregularities would be sufficient to establish that the thing in question is not a triangle as 'triangle' is used in the discourse of geometry.

 According to St. Thomas Aquinas, finite things are caused by God. They thus bear a 'likeness' to God. God's attributes are exemplary versions of the attributes possessed by finite things. We reach whatever understanding we have of God's attributes, by removing 'imperfections' that attend these qualities when possessed by finite things.[1] With respect to the predicate 'good', for example, St. Thomas

Introduction: Two Working Assumptions

writes as follows in the *Summa Theologica* (Pt. I, Q. 6, A. 4):[2]

> Each being is called good because of the divine goodness, the first exemplar principle as well as the efficient and telic cause of all goodness. Yet it is nonetheless the case that each being is called good because of a likeness of the divine goodness by which it is denominated.

Again, in *questiones disputatae de veritate* (XXI, 4) St. Thomas says:

> Every agent is found to produce effects which resemble it. Hence if the first goodness is the efficient cause of all things, it must imprint its likeness upon things which it produces. Thus each thing is called good because of an intrinsic goodness impressed upon it, and yet is further denominated good because of the first goodness which is the exemplar and efficient cause of all created goodness.

Shall we say that 'good' has the same meaning when applied to God as it has when applied to things other than God (e.g., Socrates)? As above, it seems to me that the answer we give to this question is unimportant once we get this far into the discussion. We might say that 'good' has the same meaning in the two cases, and we might say that it has a different meaning in the two cases. We might even say (as St. Thomas sometimes says) that we are here dealing with a case in which 'good' is 'midway between' having the same meaning and having different meanings in the two cases. However, as above, the following point seems to me to be important regardless of the answer one gives to the question about same or different meanings. When St. Thomas affirms that God is good, I think he means to be saying *at least as much about* God as one would say about, e.g., Socrates, if one were to affirm that Socrates is good. A study of 'good' in non-theological contexts reveals at least the minimum implications of the corresponding predication statements about God. This is to say that while Socrates is good, God is *perfectly* good. If we could find reasons sufficient for rejecting the claim that a given thing is good as 'good' is used in discourse about finite agents, these same reasons would be sufficient for rejecting the claim that the thing in question is good as 'good' is used in discourse about the nature of God. In fact, if we could find moral irregularities sufficient to cause hesitations or prompt reservations about whether a thing is good as 'good' is used in discourse about finite agents, these irregularities would be enough to establish that the agent under consideration is not good as 'good' is used in the discourse of theology.

As a general remark, I shall assume for the remainder of this essay that when theologians such as St. Augustine, Boethius, St. Thomas, St. Anselm and Frederich Schleiermacher speak of God as, e.g., good, knowledgeable, powerful, etc., the terms 'good', 'knowledgeable', 'powerful', etc., are related to their counterparts in statements such as 'Socrates is good', 'Socrates is knowledgeable', etc., in the way in which the two occurrences of 'triangle' are related in the situations described above. I shall assume, in other words, that the meta-theological position expressed by St. Thomas in the passages quoted above is a position that would be endorsed by the theologians I shall be discussing in this essay. In cases where this position is not explicitly affirmed in the writings of a given theologian, I would refer the reader to actual arguments used by the theologian when explicating and defending first-level doctrines about the nature of God. Look, for example, at St. Anselm's remarks on the question of whether God is both perfectly merciful and perfectly just (*Proslogium*, Chs. IX–XI). Though I shall not detail the import of these passages here, I am confident that but a brief review of their contents would provide assurance that for St. Anselm, analyses of 'merciful' and 'just' occurring in non-theological contexts, reveal at least the minimum implications of statements in which these terms are used to characterize God.

Though I am reasonably sure that the assumption I am here making about the meaning of positive predicate terms usually used to characterize God is an adequate reflection of the way these terms are understood by the theologians I shall be discussing, I shall not enter into a prolonged

Introduction: Two Working Assumptions

defence of this thesis. For purposes of this essay, I shall simply assume it without further argument. Among other things, this assumption will furnish the backing for arguments in which I shall first identify a condition or circumstance that would be sufficient to defeat an application of, e.g., 'knowledgeable' as it applies to Socrates and from this conclude that the same condition or circumstance would be sufficient to defeat an application of 'omniscient' (i.e., 'perfectly knowledgeable') as it applies to God. This form of argument will be prominent in Chs. 6 and 7.

NOTES

[1] In *Summa Theologica* (Pt. I, Q. 14, A. 1.) St. Thomas says:

Because perfections flowing from God to Creatures exist in a higher state in God himself, whenever a name taken from any created perfection is attributed to God, there must be separated from its signification anything that belongs to the imperfect mode proper to creatures. (This passage taken from *The Basic Writings of St. Thomas Aquinas*, ed. A. Pegis.)

[2] Both of the following passages were translated by George P. Klubertanz, S.J. *Thomas Aquinas on Analogy* (Chicago, Loyola University Press, 1960), p. 55. For a good analysis of St. Thomas's views on the topic of theological predication, see the whole of Klubertanz's discussion in Ch. III. For an enlightening discussion on how poorly St. Thomas has been understood on this topic (even by his most famous interpreters) see Klubertanz's remarks in Ch. I.

1
The Predicate 'Timeless'

In *The Christian Faith*, Frederich Schleiermacher says that God is eternal in the sense of 'timeless' ('*zeitlos*').[1] He says, too, that God is 'spaceless'.[2] Further, Schleiermacher says that timelessness and spacelessness are directly parallel concepts.[3] What one says about God *vis-à-vis* time when one says that He is timeless, is precisely what one says about God *vis-à-vis* space when one says that He is spaceless. I think it will be easier to grasp the details of the notion of timelessness if we look briefly at what Schleiermacher says in his text about the corresponding notion of spacelessness.

On Schleiermacher's account, the claim that God is spaceless involves two closely related ideas. First, God is not, as he says, 'space-filling'. This is to say that God has no spatial extension. He is not, e.g., three feet tall. Secondly, Schleiermacher says that there are no 'spatial contrasts' between God and other things. The point seems to be that God bears no special relation to other things. God is not, e.g., three feet to the left of Jones or four miles above the clouds.[4]

It is important to see that we have two distinct (though related) ideas working here. To say that God does not bear spatial contrasts with other things is not the same as to say that God is not 'space-filling'. A Euclidean point has spatial location but no spatial extension. If we could allow the possibility of there being a spatially extensionless thing (e.g., a mind or an idea), we might still insist that this thing has spatial location. (John Locke said that minds and ideas have location in space.) Thus, to say that a given thing lacks spatial extension does not commit one to the view that that thing also lacks spatial location. A thing might have spatial location without having spatial extension. However, I think that these two ideas are logically connected in the other direction. With the possible exception of the universe considered as a single unit (which requires very special treatment) if something lacks spatial location, it also lacks spatial extension. Crudely speaking, to have spatial extension is to occupy more than one spatial position at a time. Thus, we might summarize the claim that God is spaceless in the statement: 'God lacks spatial location'. This formula would probably entail that God also lacks spatial extension. For present purposes, however, I shall keep these two conceptual elements distinct. It will be to our advantage if we work with the expanded (though less elegant) version of the claim that God is spaceless.

What now of time? Following Schleiermacher's idea that spacelessness and timelessness are directly parallel concepts, we must divide the notion of timelessness into two closely related ideas. First, if God is timeless, He has no duration, i.e., He lacks temporal extension. Schleiermacher introduces this thesis by contrasting the life of God with the life of the Universe of natural objects.[5] Let it be true that the universe has a history that is indefinitely extended both forward and backward in time. The history of the universe has no temporal limits. Still the world has a history. It is, as it were, 'spread out in time'. This is what is denied of God when it is said that His life lacks duration. It is not just that the life of God lacks temporal limits: the point is that it has no temporal spread at all. Secondly, if God is timeless, God also lacks temporal location. God did not exist *before* Columbus discovered America nor will He exist *after* the turn of the century. Schleiermacher says that with respect to God, there is no 'temporal opposition of before and after'.[6] This looks to be the temporal counterpart of the idea that the life of God lacks 'spatial contrasts'. As a general comment, Schleiermacher insists that God is 'utterly timeless'[7] –

completely 'outside all contact with time'.[8] The point seems to be that God is not to be qualified by temporal predicates of any kind – neither time-extension predicates (such as, e.g., 'six years old') nor time-location predicates (such as, e.g., 'before Columbus').

Again, it is important to see that we have two distinct (though closely related) ideas operating here. Let us call the temporal counterpart of the Euclidean point a 'moment'. A moment has temporal location, but no temporal extension. Two p.m., 16 March 1822 might count as a moment. Now suppose that it makes sense to speak of a thing having momentary existence. Such a thing would have temporal location but no duration. Given this much, if we knew that a given thing lacked temporal extension, we could not conclude that it also lacked temporal location. Something might have location in time without having duration. However, as I suggested when working with the elements of the notion of spacelessness, I think that the elements of timelessness are logically related in the other direction. With the possible exception of the universe considered as a whole, if something has temporal extension, it also has temporal position. In a manner of speaking, to have duration is, simply, to occupy a number of consecutive temporal positions. Thus, the claim that God is timeless might be compressed into the single statement: 'God lacks temporal location'. But for present purposes I shall keep these two ideas distinct. We shall get a better look into the interior of timelessness if we keep its ingredients as isolated as possible.

The claim that God is timeless in the sense just outlined is rich with tradition. Keeping its two conceptual elements distinct in our minds, let us look briefly at some of its more important medieval sources.

Concerning the thesis that the life of God lacks duration (or temporal extension), consider the following somewhat vague remark from Bk. XI, Ch. 13 of St. Augustine's *Confessions*.[9]

> Thy years do not come and go; while these years of ours do come and go, in order that they all may come. All Thy years stand together

The Predicate 'Timeless'

[and in one non-extended instant], for they stand still, nor are those going away cut off by those coming, for they do not pass away, but these years of ours shall all be when they are all no more. Thy years are but one day, and Thy day is not a daily recurrent, but today. Thy present day does not give place to tomorrow, nor, indeed, does it take the place of yesterday. Thy present day is eternity.

This same theme is developed in considerably more detail and with much greater clarity in Bk. V, sec. 6 of Boethius's *Consolation*. It is taken over from Boethius by St. Thomas in Pt. I, Q. X of the *Summa Theologica*. Boethius (anticipating Schleiermacher) introduced this thesis by contrasting the life of God with the life of the Universe. Grant that the Universe has limitless temporal spread. The life of God is to be distinguished from the life of the Universe in that the former involves no temporal extension at all.

Focus now on the idea that the life of God lacks temporal location as well as temporal extension. Perhaps the clearest and most emphatic expression of this thesis is to be found in the writings of St. Anselm. In Ch. XIX of the *Proslogium*, Anselm writes:[10]

> Thou wast not, then, yesterday, nor wilt thou be tomorrow; but yesterday and today and tomorrow thou art; or, rather, neither yesterday, nor today nor tomorrow thou art; but simply, thou art, outside all time. For yesterday and today and tomorrow have no existence, except in time; but thou, although nothing exists without thee, nevertheless dost not exist in space or time, but all things exist in thee.

Again, in Ch. XXII of the *Monologium* this same point is repeated:[11]

> In no place or time, then, is this being properly said to exist, since it is contained by no other at all... [The Supreme Being has no place or time because] it has not taken to itself distinctions of place or time, neither here, nor there, nor anywhere, nor then, nor now, nor at any time; nor does it exist in terms of the fleeting present in which we live, nor has it existed, nor will it exist in terms of the past or future, since these are restricted to things finite and mutable, which it is not.

God and Timelessness

In both these passages Anselm insists that time-location predicates (as well as space-location predicates) are not to be used when characterizing God. God did not exist *before* the outbreak of civil war in America, nor will He exist after the coming election. It is never true to say that God exist*ed*, or that He *will* exist. But, further, Anselm also makes clear that God cannot be said to exist *now*. A being existing at the present moment, would be, as he says, 'contained' in time.[12]

Following Boethius, St. Thomas defines the term 'eternity' in the odd formula: 'The simultaneously-whole and perfect possession of indeterminable life.'[13] St. Thomas unfolds the implications of this definition in the following remark from the Pt. I, Q. X of the *Summa Theologica*:[14]

> Two things are to be considered in time; time itself which is successive, and the *now* of time which is imperfect. Hence, the expression *simultaneously-whole* is used to remove the idea of time, and the word *perfect* is used to exclude the *now* of time.

Thomas here seems to be making the distinction made above between the notion of temporal extension (which involves the idea of succession) and the notion of temporal location, i.e., the idea of existing at a given moment – a given 'now of time'. The latter as well as the former is denied application to God in the claim that God is eternal. St. Thomas seems to be committed to the view that with respect to any given location in time (before Columbus discovered America, after the turn of the century, right now, i.e., at the present moment) God cannot be said to exist at that time.

As regards Boethius's position on the question of God's location in time, the matter is a little less clear than it is in the case of Anselm and St. Thomas. Boethius clearly says that God cannot be located either *before* or *after* a given time or event, but there is some obscurity in his text as to whether God can be located in the temporal *present*. I should like to conclude this opening chapter with a brief examination of the sources of this obscurity. I think there is

The Predicate 'Timeless'

something important to be learned from a study of Boethius's remarks on this topic.

In Pt. V of the *Consolation*, Boethius formulates two quite different theses using two Latin locutions, both of which are generally translated into English with the help of the single term 'present'. First, Boethius says that temporal objects and events are *present* to God in the sense that he 'sees'[15] or 'beholds'[16] them, i.e., in the sense that He is directly aware of them. He says that the Supreme Being has '... an infinity of movable time present (*praesentam*) to it'.[17] I doubt that Boethius would regard this claim as relevant to the topic we are now discussing. I think he intended that it carry no implications as regards God's temporal qualities or lack thereof. Let y be a temporal object, circumstance or event and let x be some (knowing) individual who is aware of y. x might exist before y or after y (allowing the logical possibility of directly observing past or future events as in a crystal ball) and, of course, x and y might exist simultaneously. Given only that x is aware of y, one would not conclude that x exists before y; one would not conclude that x exists after y; and one would not conclude that x and y exist simultaneously. But further (and this is the point of real importance), given only that x is aware of y, one might be able to hold that x and y bear no temporal relation to one another at all. We here need a distinction between the *awareness of time* (let this phrase cover the awareness of temporal objects and events as well as the awareness of the passage of time) and the *time of awareness* (i.e., the temporal position of the awareness itself or the individual who is aware). Boethius says that God is directly aware of time and its contents, i.e., that time and its contents are present to God. But I don't think he means for us to conclude that God's awareness (or God Himself) has location in time. I think Boethius is here counting on us to make the distinction between the awareness of time and the time of awareness. (Kant made use of this distinction in the *First Critique* when discussing the relation between the Transcendental Ego and spatio-temporal phenomena. I shall say

God and Timelessness

more on this topic in the fourth, fifth and seventh chapters of this essay.)

Secondly, there are places in Boethius's texts in which he says that God 'has always an eternal and present (*praesontarius*) state'.[18] God exists in the 'eternal-present'. Augustine called this 'ever-present eternity' and the 'everlasting present'.[19] This does not seem to be a claim about God's *awareness* of temporal objects. It seems to be a comment about God's metaphysical (as opposed to epistemological) relation to time and the objects it contains. Further, this thesis is very difficult to grasp. I think that there are at least two ways in which it might be understood.

It might be that what Boethius had in mind when he said that God exists in the 'eternal-present' is that given a position at any one moment in time, one could correctly assert that God exists *now* (i.e., at this moment). This would be to deny St. Thomas's claim that God does not exist in the 'now of time'. However, if we were to accept this reading of the passages in question I think they would then conflict openly with the idea that the life of God lacks duration. If at each moment between three o'clock and four o'clock one could say, truly, that God exists *now* (i.e., at this moment), it would then follow that God exists at each moment between three o'clock and four o'clock. This would entail that the life of God *has* duration; for what is it to have duration if it is not to exist at each moment in a temporally extended interval?

On the other hand, it might be that what Boethius meant to be affirming in the passages in which he said that God exists in the 'eternal-present' is not that God exists at each moment in time, but rather that God exists in a special sense of 'exists' (or that God possesses a special mode of existence) that is unique to individuals having no location in time. Let me explain this second possibility a little further.[20]

We say that there exists a prime number between 5 and 9. Some contemporary philosophers have suggested the following account of the term 'exists' as it occurs in this

The Predicate 'Timeless'

statement. Suppose that at three o'clock I said: 'There exists a prime number between 5 and 9.' What I said was true. But it does not follow that at four o'clock the statement: 'There exist*ed* a prime number between 5 and 9' could have been uttered truly; nor does it follow that at two o'clock the statement: 'There *will* exist a prime number between 5 and 9' could have been uttered truly. There is no use for the locutions 'exist*ed*' or '*will* exist' when talking about numbers. It follows (on this account) that had I said at three o'clock that there exists a prime number between 5 and 9 *now* (meaning *at this moment*), my remark would have been incorrect. Had the prime existed at three o'clock (as would have been affirmed had I said at that time that it exists *now*), it would follow by the ordinary meaning of tensed phrases, that at two o'clock the future tense existential claim could have been made correctly and at four o'clock the past tense existential claim could have been made correctly. The conclusion is that there is a sense of 'exists' (present tense) that does not bear the usual logical relations to 'existed' (past tense) and 'will exist' (future tense). To affirm of something that it exists in this special sense of 'exists' is not to affirm that the thing in question exists in the temporal present.

Now let's suppose that Boethius was thinking of God as existing in this a-temporal sense of 'exists' (or in this a-temporal mode of existence). He might well have used terms usually reserved for marking the temporal present as ways of underscoring the idea that the sense of 'exists' involved in 'God exists' is a sense of this term that does not bear the usual logical relations to sentences utilizing past and future tenses of this term. The prime number between 5 and 9 might be characterized as 'eternally present' or as existing in an 'eternal now' meaning that whenever uttered, the claim that it *exists* (present tense) is correct, but that whenever uttered, the claim that it exist*ed* (past tense) or *will* exist (future tense) is incorrect. The phrase 'simultaneously-whole' seems to allow this sort of interpretation too. If taken literally, 'God is simultaneously-whole' would appear to mean that the life of God has temporal compactness – it occurs *all at once*. (Boethius actually says this in some places.) It would then tend to suggest that God has a single location – that He is a momentary being. But I don't think that we must read the text in this way. Boethius may have employed the phrase 'simultaneously-whole' as a way of emphasizing the idea that God exists in a sense of 'exists' that is incompatible with the concept of temporal spread. The prime number between 5 and 9 might be said to be 'simultaneously-whole' in the sense that it has no history – there are no earlier or later *parts* of its existence. Of course, if the temporal terms used by Boethius to characterize God can be interpreted as having this sort of import, then the passages in which Boethius says that God exists in the 'eternal-present', that God is 'simultaneously-whole', etc., need not be understood as assigning God location in the 'now of time'. To be sure, these passages contain locutions that suggest that God has temporal location, but on the interpretation we are now considering these locutions are being used as figurative ways of underscoring certain aspects of the idea that God exists in an a-temporal sense of the word 'exists'.

I shall not claim categorically that the second of the interpretations just suggested is the right way of understanding the passages in which Boethius says that God exists in the 'eternal-present'. I think, however, that there are at least two reasons for thinking that this is so. In the first place, it seems unlikely that a theologian of the stature of Boethius would have failed to detect the rather obvious logical conflict that would have resulted had he claimed both that the life of God lacks duration and that God is temporally present at each moment in time. The first interpretation of these passages thus seems initially implausible. It would require that we accuse Boethius of what would appear to be a relatively simple logical error regarding the conceptual connection between existing at a number of consecutive temporal locations and having duration. Secondly, Boethius explicitly says that the concept of eternity he is employing in his text is one that he borrowed from Plato.[21] Now, to be sure, Plato's remarks on the topic of eternity are not paradigms of precision and clarity, but I think that it is worth noting that in the *Timaeus* (at least), Plato says that if something is eternal, one cannot say that it *was* or that it *will be*, but only that it *is*. He writes:[22]

> ... 'was' and 'will be' are created species of time which we in our carelessness mistakenly apply to eternal being. For we say that it was, is, and will be; but, in truth, 'is' applies to it, while 'was' and 'will be' are properly said of becoming in time. They are motions, but that which is immovably the same for ever cannot become older or younger in time.

As was suggested above, if something *is*, but is such that it is never correct to say that it *was*, or that it *will be*, it *is* in a sense of '*is*' that does not mean 'is now'. If something *is now*, then it *is* in a sense of '*is*' for which there will be times when it is correct to say that it *was* and that it *will be*. The object in question must exist in an a-temporal sense of 'exists'.

Schleiermacher said that God is eternal in the sense of timeless, i.e., that the life of God lacks temporal position and temporal extension. St. Thomas also held this view and I think that a sympathetic interpretation of the passages referred to above from Boethius's *Consolation* would attribute this position to him as well. In the *Confessions*, St. Augustine said that God lacks temporal extension and that He exists in 'ever-present eternity'. I am inclined to interpret these remarks as I interpreted similar remarks of Boethius above. Lastly, Anselm emphasized that God lacks temporal location. Considerations of consistency would commit him to the idea that God also lacks temporal extension. That God is timeless in the sense outlined in the fourth paragraph of this chapter would thus appear to be a doctrine that has been endorsed by a number of important figures in the history of Christian theology.

NOTES

[1] *The Christian Faith*, numbered para. 52, sec. 1. English translation of the second edition, ed. by H. R. Mackintosh and J. S. Stewart, Edinburgh, Clark, 1956; pp. 203–5.

[2] *Ibid.*, numbered para. 53, sec. 1, pp. 206–8.

[3] *Ibid.*

[4] *Ibid.*, numbered para. 53, sec. 2, p. 209.

[5] *Ibid.*, numbered para. 52, secs. 1 and 2, pp. 204–5.

[6] *Ibid.*

[7] *Ibid.*

[8] *Ibid.*, numbered para. 41, sec. 1, p. 154.

[9] This passage translated by V. J. Bourke, New York (*Fathers of the Church*), The Catholic University of America Press, 1953, pp. 342–3. The phrase in brackets is added by Bourke in an explanatory footnote.

[10] This passage translated by Sidney Deane, *St. Anselm*, La Salle, Court, 1958, p. 25.

[11] *Ibid.*, p. 81. (In the first section of Ch. 7, I cite and discuss those portions of this passage that I have here omitted.)

[12] *Monologium*, Ch. XXIII, Deane, p. 83.

[13] See *Consolation*, Bk. V, sec. 6, ll. 9–11. *Boethius*, translated by H. F. Stewart and E. K. Rand, Cambridge, Harvard University Press, 1962, p. 401. Anselm also used this formula. See *Monologium*, Ch. XXIV, Deane, p. 83.

[14] Article 1, reply to objection 5. This passage taken from *The Basic Writings of St. Thomas*, ed. A. C. Pegis, New York, Random House, 1945, p. 75.

[15] *Consolation*, ll. 140–60. Stewart and Rand translation, p. 409.

[16] *Ibid.*, l. 176, p. 411.

[17] *Ibid.*, Bk. V, sec. 6, ll. 32–4, p. 401.

[18] *Ibid.*, ll. 61–2, p. 403.

[19] *Confessions*, Tr. V. J. Bourke, Bk. XI, Ch. 13 (fifth paragraph) and Ch. 11 (second paragraph).

[20] For what follows in the next three paragraphs, I am indebted to suggestions made by William Kneale in his article 'Time and Eternity in Theology', *Proceedings of the Aristotelian Society*, 1961, especially sec. III; and to G. E. L. Owen in his article, 'Plato and Parmenides on the Timeless Present', *Monist*, 1966.

[21] *Consolation*, l. 36, Stewart and Rand translation, p. 401. I am indebted to Mrs. Marilyn McCord Adams for pointing out the importance of this reference to Plato.

[22] *Timaeus*, 37E6–38A6. This passage translated by William Kneale, 'Time and Eternity in Theology', pp. 92–3.

2
The Logical Status of 'God is Timeless'

In this chapter I shall try to identify the general logical status of the statement 'God is timeless'. I shall restrict attention to cases in which this statement occurs in theological texts such as those mentioned in the last chapter. In order to avoid complications that would arise were we to consider formulations of this statement that entail the existence of God, I shall also restrict attention to the hypothetical function 'If x is God, then x is timeless'. I want to ask whether propositions fitting this form are necessary truths.

I

In this first section of the present chapter I shall explicate and evaluate a doctrine that I shall refer to as 'the doctrine of essential predication'. In this discussion, the term 'God' will be used as an individual designator carrying nothing in the way of semantical import. In the first chapter of *A System of Logic*, J. S. Mill said that proper names do not have meaning – in the usual sense of 'meaning'. For purposes of this opening discussion, I shall assume that 'God' is a proper name of the sort described by Mill: it is an alternative name for the individual whose other name is 'Yahweh'. Further, I shall assume that the individual designated by the term 'God' (if there is one) is eternal, omnipotent, omniscient, perfectly good, etc. These are things that we know about him – perhaps from revelation. For the moment I am supposing that the individual whose name is 'God' (if He exists) has the qualities usually assigned to Him in traditional theological literature, but I am also supposing that the predicate-terms normally used to designate these qualities are not attached to the term 'God' by logical or semantical connections. The function 'If x is God, then x is eternal (omnipotent, etc.)' will be treated as grammatically similar to the function 'If x is Jones, then x is a tall man with a black moustache'.

(*a*) Medieval theologians sometimes converted attribute terms such as 'good' and 'wise' into nouns such as 'goodness' and 'wisdom' asserting what would appear to be an identity relation between God and the attribute in question. It was affirmed, for example, that God *is* Goodness and that God *is* Wisdom. The following line of reasoning was often used to justify this way of talking.

Socrates is good. But goodness is not part of the 'essence' of Socrates. While Socrates is good, we could imagine or conceive of him as other than good. Goodness is (so to speak) 'detachable' from Socrates – it is *added to*, or 'super-added', to the individual whose name is Socrates. This idea is mirrored in the form of words we use when assigning goodness to Socrates: we say 'Socrates is good' meaning 'Socrates *has* or *possesses* goodness'. The picture conveyed is one in which Socrates stands on one side of the fence and an attribute that *belongs to him*, but that is 'detachable' from him, stands on the other. Now this latter is an image we want to avoid when speaking of God and his goodness. Goodness is not 'detachable' from God – it qualifies his 'essence'. Goodness is not 'superadded' to the individual named 'God'. God would not be the individual He is if He were other than perfectly good.[1] But, as was suggested by St. Anselm in the sixteenth chapter of the *Monologium*, if we are to avoid the picture of God as somehow separable from his attributes, we must avoid the form of words that encourages this picture. Thus, as Anselm proposes, when we say that God is good, we should not read this as meaning 'God *possesses* goodness'. We should read this as meaning 'God *is* Goodness'. St. Augustine maps out the whole programme in the following passage from Bk. XI, Ch. 10 of the *City of God*:[2]

> ... the nature of the Trinity is called simple, because it has not anything which it can lose, and because it is not one thing and its contents another, as a cup of liquor, or a body and its colour, or the air and the light or heat of it, or a mind and its wisdom. For none of these is what it has: the cup is not liquor, nor the body colour, nor the air light and heat, nor the mind wisdom. And hence they can be deprived of what they have, and can be turned or changed into other qualities and states, so that the cup may be emptied of the liquor of which it is full, the body discoloured, the air darken, the mind grow silly ... According to this, then, those things which are essential and truly divine are called simple, because in them quality and substance are identical and because they are divine, or wise, or blessed in themselves, and without extraneous supplement.

With respect to a body and its colour Augustine says that the colour can be lost and the body remain the body (substance) it was. In this case, it is not true that the body 'is what it has' ('*est id quod habet*'). Its identity as the thing it is is not tied up with its being a given colour. But the situation is otherwise as regards God and, e.g., goodness. In this case, the identity of the individual is connected with its being good. St. Augustine says that with respect to God, the being 'has not anything it can lose' ('*cui non sit aliquid habere, quod vel possit amittere*'). It 'is what it has'. The conclusion drawn is that in the case of God, 'the quality and the substance are identical'. Following Anselm we should say 'God *is* Goodness' rather than 'God *possesses* goodness'.

The medieval theologians who held that God is identical with each of His attributes often drew out the implications of this idea in considerable detail. If God is identical with, e.g., goodness, and if God is also identical with, e.g., wisdom, then goodness and wisdom must be identical with one another (by the transitivity of the identity relation).[3] What does this mean? I'm not really sure; but I think that at least part of the point can be formulated in the following series of entailment relations. If we know of a given individual that it is God, then we can conclude (rigorously) that that individual is perfectly good. If we know that a given individual is perfectly good, we can conclude (rigorously) that that individual is God. Since the same can be said of God and, e.g., perfect wisdom, it follows that if we know that a given individual is perfectly good, we can conclude (rigorously) that that individual is perfectly wise and vice versa. Thus 'x is God' entails 'x is perfectly good' and 'x is perfectly wise'; 'x is perfectly good' entails 'x is God' and 'x is perfectly wise'; and 'x is perfectly wise' entails 'x is God' and 'x is perfectly good'. In his textbook of scholastic theology, Father Joseph Pohle summarizes this point as follows:[4]

> ... each separate divine perfection logically postulates every other divine perfection because all of God's perfections are identical among themselves and with His essence and existence.

I shall not try to uncover all of the assumptions underlying the various steps of this complex line of reasoning. I want to deal with just one of the themes contained in the sequence, *viz.*, that from propositions of the form 'x is God', one can infer (rigorously) 'x is perfectly good', 'x is perfectly wise', etc. (This thesis must be distinguished from the claim that all of the divine attributes are the same, i.e., that each of the divine attributes entails one another. It must also be distinguished from the claim that from each proposition of the form 'x is pefectly wise', 'x is perfectly good', etc., one can infer 'x is God'.) It seems to me that this theme is closely related to the major point made by Augustine in the passage quoted above. On Augustine's account the being that is God 'is what it has': the being that is God 'has not anything it can lose'. I want to expand this idea in such a way as to make clear how it supports inferences from 'x is God' to 'x is perfectly good', 'x is perfectly wise', etc.

Let us suppose that each of the quality terms 'eternity', 'omnipotence', 'omniscience', 'perfect goodness', etc., is so

The Logical Status of 'God is Timeless'

related to the concept *being* (object, individual, thing) or *same being* (same object, same individual, same thing) that if a given being is, e.g., perfectly good, that being would not have been the being it is had it not been perfectly good. This is to say that the question of whether a given individual is, e.g., perfectly good, is a question about the *identity* of the individual in question. 'Perfect goodness' and 'same individual' are so connected that if a given individual is perfectly good, that individual would not have been *that* individual had it not been perfectly good. I shall refer to this as 'the doctrine of essential predication'.

It should be clear that the doctrine I have just put forward is one in which it is claimed that there is a certain logical relation between the concept *being* (or same being) on the one hand, and each of the concepts *eternity, omnipotence, perfect goodness,* etc., on the other hand. This doctrine is most clearly stated in the formal, rather than the material mode of speech – i.e., it is most clearly stated as a theory about the relations between concepts or meanings, rather than a theory about the features of concrete individuals. However, I shall not hesitate to apply the theory using the material, rather than the formal mode of speech. I shall sometimes say that, e.g., *perfect goodness* (the feature) is an 'essential property' of any *individual* possessing it. When I do this, the reader should understand that I am using this material locution as a way of making a comment about the logical relations between, e.g., 'perfectly good' and 'being' (or 'same being').

The following passage is taken from J. N. Findlay's article 'Can God's Existence be Disproved?'[5]

> It is contrary to the demands inherent in religious attitudes that their object... should possess its various excellences in some merely adventitious or contingent manner. It would be quite unsatisfactory from a religious standpoint, if an object merely happened to be wise, good, powerful and so forth, even to the superlative degree... We might respect this object as the crowning instance of most excellent qualities, but we should incline our head before the qualities and not before the person... for though such qualities might

be intimately characteristic of the Supreme Being, they still wouldn't be inalienably his own... Wisdom, kindness and other excellences deserve respect wherever they are manifested, but no being can appropriate them as its personal perquisites, even if it does possess them in superlative degree. And so we are led irresistibly by the demands inherent in religious reverence, to hold that an adequate object of worship must possess its various qualities in *some necessary manner*.

God is perfectly good. On Findlay's account, God must possess perfect goodness 'in some necessary manner'. Perfect goodness must be (as Findlay says) 'inalienably His own'. These remarks fit in well with the comments made above. On the doctrine of essential predication, if a given individual is perfectly good, that individual possesses perfect goodness 'in some necessary manner'. This is to say that if a given individual is perfectly good, that individual could not have failed to be perfectly good. Any individual lacking perfect goodness could not have been *that* individual. In similar fashion, if perfect goodness is an essential property of any individual possessing it, then if a given individual is perfectly good, perfect goodness is 'inalienably his own'. It is not possible that a perfectly good individual should become 'alienated' from (i.e., lose) perfect goodness. A perfectly good being could not *cease* to be perfectly good. An individual loses (ceases to have, becomes alienated from) a given quality when that individual possesses that quality at a given time and lacks that quality at a later time. But if perfect goodness is an essential property of any individual possessing it, no individual could be perfectly good at a given time and not perfectly good at a later time. If a given individual is perfectly good at a given time, then any individual lacking perfect goodness at a later time could not be *that* individual. I think that this was the point St. Augustine was making when he said that the Supreme Being 'has not anything it can lose'. Though a body may lose its colour and remain the individual it is, the qualities possessed by God are such that no individual could lose them without losing its identity.

The Logical Status of 'God is Timeless'

Up to this point, it would appear that the thesis Findlay reports in the passage cited above is precisely the one I have introduced under the title 'the doctrine of essential predication'. However, there is a discrepancy here that must not go unnoticed. Findlay says that some being might possess, e.g., perfect goodness, in some 'merely adventitious and contingent manner'. The doctrine that I have sketched does not provide for this possibility. Socrates possesses goodness in some 'merely adventitious and contingent manner'. But Socrates is not *perfectly* good. On the doctrine I have outlined, perfect goodness is an essential property of *every* individual possessing it. No being could *just happen* to be perfectly good. This claim rests on a general theory about the logical relation between 'being' (or 'same being') on the one hand, and 'perfectly good' on the other. I have not been able to formulate a theory in accordance with which it would be possible that some beings possess perfect goodness 'in some necessary manner' and some beings possess it in some 'contingent' manner. Unless we are supposing a perfectly general conceptual connection between 'perfect goodness' and 'being' (or 'same being'), I can attach no meaning to the claim that *any* being possesses perfect goodness 'in some necessary manner'.

I think I can now make clear the central point I want to abstract from this discussion. It concerns the logical status of the hypothetical function 'If x is God, then x is perfectly good'.

Suppose the police files tell us that Jones (if he is still alive) is a tall man with a black moustache. While acknowledging that Jones (if he is alive) has a black moustache, we could conceive of the case in which a certain individual is Jones though that individual does not have a black moustache. We could imagine Jones without his black moustache. However, the situation seems to be otherwise as regards individuals and their essential properties. We are supposing that God (if He exists) is perfectly good. This is something we have been given in revelation. If perfect goodness is an essential property of any individual possessing it, we could not conceive of the case in which a given individual is God (the one mentioned in the revelation) though that individual is not perfectly good. On the doctrine of essential predication, if a given individual is perfectly good, one could not imagine that individual as other than perfectly good. To imagine someone devoid of perfect goodness would be to imagine someone other than the given individual. Thus, if we assume that God (if He exists) is perfectly good and if we also assume that perfect goodness is an essential property of any individual possessing it, the hypothetical function 'If x is God, then x is perfectly good' must be assigned the status of a necessary truth.

Shall we say that the necessity of the function 'If x is God then x is perfectly good' results from the meaning of the words it employs? Is it, in other words, an *analytic* truth? I think that there are two ways of approaching this question.

On the one hand, I think it is clear that given the doctrine of essential predication, if it is specified that the individual named 'God' (if He exists) is perfectly good, the necessity of 'If x is God, then x is perfectly good' in no way depends on the fact that we have designated the individual of whom we are speaking with the special term 'God'. We would get the same result had we called him 'Yahweh' or, for that matter, 'Halifax' or 'Susan'. If we were told that an individual named 'Halifax' (if he exists) is perfectly good, then if perfect goodness is an essential property of any individual possessing it, the function 'If x is Halifax, then x is perfectly good' would have to be counted as a necessary truth. Under these conditions, if we were to conceive of some individual as other than perfectly good, we would be conceiving of some individual other than the one under consideration – the one who has been called 'Halifax'. When looked at in this way, it would appear that the necessity of the function 'If x is God, then x is perfectly good' does not result from the meanings of the terms occurring within it. The necessity of the function seems to depend in no way on the particularities of the subject term occurring in its antecedent.

The Logical Status of 'God is Timeless'

However, there is a second way of understanding the matter. In his article 'Proper Names', John Searle writes as follows concerning the proper name 'Aristotle':[6]

> So, if we came to agreement in advance of using the name on precisely what characteristics constituted the identity of Aristotle, our rules for using the name would be precise. But this precision would be achieved only at the cost of entailing some specific predicates by a referring use of the name. Indeed, the name itself would become superfluous for it would become logically equivalent to this set of descriptions. But if this were the case we would be in the position of only being able to refer to an object by describing it ... If the criteria for proper names were in all cases quite rigid and specific, then a proper name would be nothing more than a shorthand for these criteria, a proper name would function exactly like an elaborate definite description.

Searle says that if we could reach agreement about the features that are tied up with the identity of the individual named 'Aristotle' (i.e., Aristotle's essential properties) then the proper name 'Aristotle' would become a shorthand way of mentioning this list of features. The suggestion, seems to be that if, e.g., having brown hair could be counted as one of Aristotle's essential properties, then the proper name 'Aristotle' would in part *mean* 'a brown-haired individual' and the statement 'Aristotle has brown hair' (read hypothetically) would be an analytic truth. If we could accept this theory of meaning as regards proper names, then if perfect goodness could be taken as an essential property of the individual God (if He exists), the proper name 'God' would in part *mean* 'a perfectly good individual' and the statement 'God is perfectly good' (read hypothetically) would have to be counted as a necessary truth. On this analysis, the necessity of the function 'If x is God, then x is perfectly good' could be analysed as resulting from the meanings of the terms occurring within it. It would have to be counted as an analytic truth.

It is not important that we reach agreement on the question before us. In a theology in which the doctrine of essential predication is affirmed, statements such as 'God is perfectly good', 'God is perfectly wise', etc., are necessary truths grounded ultimately in conceptual connections, whether or not we think of their necessity as resulting from the meanings of the terms they employ. (I am here assuming that 'God' works in these sentences as a proper name and that each of these sentences is interpreted as having hypothetical structure.)

(*b*) When formulated as a general theory about the logical relations between 'being' (or 'same being') and each of the predicate-terms traditionally used to characterize God, the doctrine of essential predication may well be false. In the fourth chapter of his *Religious Belief*, C. B. Martin says that even if we agree that God exists and is perfectly good, we can still *conceive* of this individual as other than perfectly good.[7] If Martin is right about this, then 'perfectly good' and 'being' (or 'same being') are not connected in the way described in the doctrine of essential predication. At the end of the fourth chapter of this essay, I shall suggest a similar view as regards the attribute of omniscience. It is not at all clear that if a given individual is omniscient, that individual would not have been the individual it is, had it not been omniscient. However, it seems to me that the matter may very well be otherwise as regards the attribute of eternity, understood as timelessness. Let me elaborate this point.

In the *Guide to the Perplexed*, Moses Maimonides says that the negations involved in the negative predicates usually assigned to God must be understood as what philosophers sometimes describe as 'type' or 'categorical' negations. Maimonides writes:[8]

> Even these negative attributes must not be formed and applied to God, except in the way in which, as you know, sometimes an attribute is made negative in reference to a thing although that attribute can naturally never be applied to it in the same sense, e.g., we say 'this wall cannot see'.

I think that the point is this: when we say of a wall that it cannot see, we do not mean to be asserting of the wall what we assert of a man when we say that the man cannot see. When I say of Jones (who is blind) that he cannot see, I am affirming that the statement, 'Jones can see', is false, i.e., that Jones is blind. But when I say of the wall that it cannot see, I do not mean to be asserting that the wall is blind. The wall is not of a type or kind that might see. I am affirming that the wall is not of a kind of which the predicate 'sighted' might be applied. The statement: 'The wall sees', is not just false; it is conceptually deficient. It is a special kind of nonsense having its source in a special kind of grammatical mix-up.

After affirming that negative predicates as a group are to be read as having categorical import when used to characterize God, Maimonides applies this point in the case of negative temporal qualifiers. With respect to the predicate 'first' and the predicate 'eternal' (understood as meaning 'endless duration' rather than 'timeless') Maimonides says that both expressions . . .

> . . . are equally inadmissible in reference to any being to which the attribute of time is not applicable, just as we do not say 'crooked' or 'straight' in reference to taste or 'salted' or 'insipid' in reference to voice.[9]

The claim is, I think, that if a being lacks position in time (i.e., is such that an 'attribute of time is not applicable'), then to assign either temporal location ('first') or duration ('eternal') to such a being is to fall into a special kind of grammatical error. To speak of a timeless being as having temporal location or duration is not just a case of assigning the *wrong* predicate; it is a case of assigning the wrong *kind* of predicate to the individual in question.

Is this right? I should think that the test of Maimonides' general thesis would require a consideration of God's negative attributes one at a time. When it is claimed that God is, e.g., immutable, should this be understood as affirming that God is not of a *type* to which change-predicates (such as, e.g., 'changed his mind', 'became aware', etc.) apply? I don't know the answer to this question – though I shall say something that will relate to this topic in Chs. 3 and 9 of this essay. However, when dealing with the predicate 'timeless', it seems to me that Maimonides' way of understanding the negative predicates that attach to God has a certain very clear attraction. The difference between a timeless being and a temporal being is a difference that crosses fundamental divisions of our ordinary conceptual scheme. On the doctrine of essential predication, this division is recorded in a claim about the identity-conditions of individuals. It is logically impossible that a timeless being should have been a temporal being. Maimonides is suggesting that this division should be marked with a heavier line. On his account, not only would it have been impossible for a timeless being to have been a temporal being, a timeless being could not have been even of a *type* with a temporal being. This is to say that the description of a timeless being that makes use of temporal predicates is not just false – and not just logically false. It is an employment of words that can be assigned no sense whatsoever. This may well be right.

For the remainder of this essay I shall assume that the intuition underpinning Maimonides' remarks on this issue is sound enough to support the (weaker) thesis expressed in the claim that timelessness is an essential property of any individual possessing it.

II

In the preceding discussion, we have worked within the confines of the assumption that the term 'God' is a proper name bearing no semantical import (except, perhaps, a semantical import acquired in the special way suggested in the passage cited from Searle). I now want to replace this assumption with two other assumptions that seem to me to more adequately reflect the actual use of 'God' as this term occurs in the ordinary and technical (theological) discourse of the Christian religion. The first assumption concerns the syntactical status of 'God' and the second assumption concerns the semantical import of this term.

The Logical Status of 'God is Timeless'

(*a*) Contemporary philosophers of religion have had a good deal to say about the syntactical status of the term 'God'. Some have said that as used in the discourse of religion, 'God' is a descriptive expression having unique reference – as is, e.g., the phrase 'the tallest man in the world'. This view has considerable attraction. The statement 'Yahweh is God' seems to be a case in which 'God' operates as a descriptive expression. This statement has the syntactical 'feel' of a statement such as 'George is the tallest man in the world'. On the other hand, there have been philosophers who have suggested that 'God' works in the discourse of religion as a proper name (as was assumed above). Again, this view has some appeal. The statements, 'God spoke to Moses' and 'God, have mercy on my soul', have the syntactical flavour of statements such as 'George spoke to Helen' and 'George, please don't call me names'.

For the remainder of this essay, I shall assume that 'God' is a descriptive expression rather than a proper name. However, in order to take account of the intuitive plausibility of the proper-name analysis of this term, I shall assume that 'God' is a special kind of descriptive expression, *viz.*, what I shall call a 'title-phrase'. Grammatically, title-phrases are descriptive expressions that often do the work of proper names and that often appear in linguistic environments similar to those associated with proper names. Let me elaborate this last remark.

For four generations after the rule of Julius Caesar, the term 'Caesar' functioned as the title of the individual who occupied the position of Emperor of Rome. The statement 'Hadrian is Caesar' was used to affirm that the individual whose name is 'Hadrian' occupies the position of Emperor of Rome. 'Caesar' in 'Hadrian is Caesar' should be classified as a descriptive expression. The sentence as a whole described Hadrian as the one who occupies the position of Emperor. Now consider the statements: 'Caesar went riding in the afternoon' and 'Caesar, I should like to have you meet my brother'. Assuming that Hadrian is Caesar (i.e., is Emperor of Rome), the first of these statements is one in which Hadrian is referred to, and the second is one in which Hadrian is addressed (rather than referred to) by his title. Of course, in both of these cases, 'Caesar' occurs in the grammatical slot that would normally be occupied by a proper name. It also looks like a proper name in that it is a singular referring expression occurring without an article. Should we say that it *is* a proper name? There seems to me to be two reasons why we should not: (1) 'Caesar' in 'Hadrian is Caesar' is not a proper name. Considerations of coherence would thus suggest that 'Caesar' in 'Caesar went riding in the afternoon' ought not to be classified as a proper name either. (2) 'Caesar' applied to Hadrian by virtue of the fact that he occupied the special position of Emperor. Given a linguistic community in which 'Caesar' in 'Hadrian is Caesar' is well understood, if one were to refer to or address an individual as 'Caesar', one would communicate (though, perhaps, one would not assert in the narrow sense) that the individual of whom, or to whom, one is speaking is Emperor of Rome. Though 'Caesar' in 'Caesar went riding in the afternoon' looks like a proper name, it carries the descriptive import that attends it in 'Hadrian is Caesar'. There thus appears to be an important contrast between 'Caesar' in 'Caesar went riding in the afternoon' and an ordinary proper name such as 'Hadrian'. 'Hadrian' did not apply to Hadrian by virtue of the fact that he occupied the special position of Emperor. In referring to or addressing Hadrian as 'Hadrian', one would not have communicated the fact that the individual of whom, or to whom, one is speaking is Emperor of Rome.

In the Judeo-Christian religious tradition, the name of the individual who is God is 'Yahweh'. In the Christian tradition, the individual whose name is 'Jesus' is also described as God. Now, most atheists would agree that Jesus existed. They would insist, however, that Jesus was not God. I could also imagine an atheist affirming that Yahweh exists – just as one might admit that a mountain or a tree worshipped by the pagans exists. In this sort of case, the difference between the religious believer and the religious non-believer would

The Logical Status of 'God is Timeless'

not emerge over the question of whether Yahweh exists. It would emerge over the question of whether Yahweh is God. Let's then ask what it is to say that Yahweh (or Jesus) is God. Some theologians have said that 'God' means 'the Ruler' (or Creator) of the Universe.[10] On this account, 'Yahweh is God' would mean that the individual named Yahweh functions in a certain capacity with respect to other individuals, *viz.*, He rules (or was the Creator of) the universe. Other theologians have claimed that 'God' means 'a being a greater than which cannot be conceived'. Given this second proposal, 'Yahweh is God' would mean that Yahweh has a certain rank or status *vis-à-vis* the individuals in the domain of actual and possible objects. (I think it is interesting to note that these two analyses have very different messages. On the first, 'God' is like 'commanding officer' – it signifies a function but not a rank. On the second, 'God' is like 'Four Star General' – it signifies a rank but not a function.) Of course, I should like very much to discover which (if either) of these two analyses is correct. But I shall not attempt to choose between them here. The point in which I am presently interested is this: 'God' in 'Yahweh is God' seems to operate as a descriptive expression marking some functional position (Ruler of the Universe) or some value-rank (a being a greater than which cannot be conceived) or some such. The sentence as a whole is one in which the individual whose name is 'Yahweh' is described as occupying this position or as having that special value-rank. 'God' in 'Yahweh is God' thus seems to be similar in important respects to 'Caesar' in 'Hadrian is Caesar'.

What then of the sentences that have led some philosophers to think that 'God' is a proper name? In the sentences: 'God spoke to Moses' and 'God, have mercy on my soul', 'God' occupies the place that might well be occupied by a proper name. It also looks like a proper name in that it is a singular referring expression occurring without an article.[11] Should we say that it *is* a proper name? I think that the same two reasons given above when discussing the syntactical status of 'Caesar' in 'Caesar went riding in the afternoon' dictate that we should not. (1) Considerations of coherence are relevant. 'God' in 'Yahweh is God' does not seem to be a proper name: it would be strange if it were a proper name in 'God spoke to Moses'. (2) Unless one is speaking obliquely – as in cases where one speaks in jest or irony, or in cases where one is describing the beliefs of others, e.g., 'God [according to the Christians] is omnipotent', or '[It is believed that] God is omnipotent' – one applies the term 'God' to a given individual when one wants to communicate the idea that the individual in question functions in a certain capacity or has a certain rank or status. To refer to or address an individual as 'God' is to communicate (though, perhaps, not to assert in the narrow sense) that the individual of whom, or to whom, he is speaking functions in that capacity or has that rank or status. Proper names do not carry this sort of import nor do they do this sort of job. In referring to, or addressing an individual as 'Jesus' or 'Yahweh', one does not communicate the idea that the individual referred to or addressed functions in some special capacity or has some special rank. This is the difference that leads me to think that although 'God' in 'God spoke to Moses' and 'God, have mercy on my soul' looks like and occupies the place of a proper name, it is not to be classified together with such terms as 'Jesus' or 'Yahweh'. 'God' does more than would, e.g., 'Yahweh' in '. . . spoke to Moses', just as 'Caesar' does more than would, e.g., 'Hadrian' in '. . . went riding in the afternoon'.

I have benefited greatly from the following remarks of Father Norris Clarke on the topic of whether 'God' is to be thought of as a description or as a proper name:[12]

> In the case of ordinary terms in the language, one must indeed choose between these two uses. But it is just one of the unusual features of this most unusual of terms, 'God' that it combines the two functions indissolubly. I would say that in view of its actual use down the ages in Western religious discourse (monotheistic for many centuries), it functions primarily as a description, but . . . this particular descriptive term can also be, and traditionally has been, used as a direct form of address or as a proper name.

The Logical Status of 'God is Timeless'

Father Clarke concludes:

> In the case of 'God', it seems to me that any adequate analysis of the role played by the term must indissolubly join these two uses: description and proper name.

On the analysis I have sketched, 'God' (like 'Caesar') is a title-term. Titles are expressions that sometimes perform the function of a proper name and sometimes appear in linguistic settings that make it difficult to distinguish them from proper names. But titles ought not to be thought of as proper names. They carry elements of meaning that make it advisable to classify them as descriptive terms. This analysis seems to me to take account of Father Clarke's intuitions concerning the use of 'God' in traditional religious discourse.

(*b*) Up to this point I have been concerned to identify and elaborate the assumption I shall be employing in the remainder of this essay about the *syntactical* status of the term 'God'. However, in the course of my deliberations I have mentioned two possible *semantical* analyses of this term, *viz.*, 'Ruler (or Creator) of the Universe' and 'a being a greater than which cannot be conceived'. I have made no commitment as to which (if either) of these semantical analyses is correct. I now want to assume that whatever may be the true account of the meaning of 'God', its semantical import is such that the quality-terms 'perfectly good', 'omnipotent', 'omniscient', etc., attach to it in such a way as to render propositions of the form, 'If x is God, then x is perfectly good', 'If x is God, then x is omnipotent', etc., necessary truths. It is a logically necessary condition of bearing the title 'God' (e.g., it is a logically necessary condition of being 'Ruler of the Universe' or a being than which no greater can be conceived) that the individual bearing the title be perfectly good, omnipotent, omniscient and the like. If we could assume that in order to be Emperor (as opposed to Empress) of Rome it is required that one be male (as opposed to female), then if 'Caesar' means 'Emperor of

Rome', the statement: 'If x is Caesar, then x is male' would have precisely the same logical status as the one I am here assuming for 'If x is God, then x is perfectly good', 'If x is God, then x is omnipotent', etc.

In most standard theological texts such as the ones discussed in Ch. 1 of this essay, statements of the form, 'If x is God, then x is ϕ' (where 'God' is read as a descriptive expression and where 'ϕ' takes attributes such as perfect goodness, omnipotence, omniscience, etc., as values), are offered as necessary truths. But, of course, 'If x is God, then x is eternal' is a proposition of this form. In these contexts, this statement must be counted as a necessary truth. In a theological context in which the predicate 'eternal' is interpreted to mean 'timeless', the statement: 'If x is God, then x is timeless' must then be counted as a necessary truth.

III

We have now developed two quite distinct lines of thinking about the logical status of propositions having the form, 'If x is God, then x is timeless'. I now want to bring these two lines together into a single view.

Let us suppose that we are dealing with a theological text in which it is claimed that the individual that is God (if there is one) is timeless. We make no assumptions about the semantical import of the term 'God'. For purposes of discussion, we assume that this term is a pure designator – a proper name of the sort described by John Stuart Mill in the first chapter of *A System of Logic*. Given this approach to the text, we would probably have to count 'If x is God, then x is timeless' as a necessary truth. This would be clear in a theology in which the doctrine of essential predication is either explicitly or implicitly asserted (as it would be in St. Augustine's or St. Anselm's texts where it is claimed that God is identical with each of his attributes), but it would be reasonable to suppose that this would be true in other cases as well. Regardless of what one thinks of the

The Logical Status of 'God is Timeless'

doctrine of essential predication when applied with respect to such predicates as 'perfectly good', 'omnipotent', etc., it is likely that if a theologian holds that God is timeless, he regards timelessness as an essential property of the individual that is God.

Now let's suppose that we are dealing with the theological text just mentioned, but let us suppose that the term 'God' operates in that text as a kind of title applying to an individual only if that individual occupies some functional position (Ruler of the Universe) or has some special value-status (e.g., a being a greater than which cannot be conceived). Let us also assume that in the text before us, it is held that the possession of timelessness is a logically necessary condition of bearing the title 'God'. Again, it will follow that the function, 'If x is God, then x is timeless' has the form of a necessary truth. This time, the necessity of the function is grounded in a semantical connection between the title-term 'God' and the predicate 'eternal' read as 'timeless', rather than in a claim about the identity-implications of possessing the attribute of timelessness.

In a theological system such as the one developed by St. Augustine or St. Anselm, timelessness is probably to be treated as an essential property of any individual possessing it. It would also be held that the predicate 'timeless' is logically connected to the title-term 'God' in the manner outlined in the last section. The statement: 'If x is God, then x is timeless' would count as a necessary truth for *both* of the reasons just mentioned. I suspect that this is true in most of the theological systems in which it is claimed that God is timeless. In a case of this sort, the full account of the logical elements operative in 'God is timeless' requires the following rather complicated formula. ('N' means 'necessarily' or 'it could not fail that'):

$N(x)$ (If x is God, then $N(x$ lacks temporal position and temporal extension)).

This formula should be read as follows:

It could not fail that the individual that is God could not fail to lack temporal position and temporal extension.

The first 'could not fail' in this statement results from an (alleged) meaning connection between the predicate 'timeless' and the title-term 'God'. The second 'could not fail' results from the (alleged) fact that timelessness is an essential property of any individual possessing it. The statement as a whole tells us that it is a logically necessary condition of bearing the title 'God' that an individual be essentially timeless, i.e., that an individual be such that it could not (logically) be a temporal being.

NOTES

[1] St. Thomas Aquinas is typical of the theologians I am here discussing. Thomas says that 'good', 'wise', etc., 'signify the divine substance'. They apply, as he says, 'substantially to God' (*Summa Theo.*, Pt. I, Q. 3, A. 2). The point is that 'good', 'wise', etc., apply to the substance (thing, individual) that is God. Further, Thomas says that the terms 'Good', 'Wise', etc., signify the 'essence' of the substance (individual) that is God. They apply 'essentially' to God (*Summa Theo.*, Pt. I, Q. 3, A. 3 and 7). Now, according to St. Thomas, we identify the 'essence' of Man when we specify those qualities an object must possess in order to count as a man. These are the qualities that must be mentioned in the definition of the class-term 'man' (*Summa Theo.*, Pt. I, Q. 3, A. 3. See also Ch. 2, last five paragraphs and Ch. 6, first paragraph of Thomas's *Being and Essence*). When we turn to the task of specifying the 'essence' of a particular individual (such as God) instead of a species such as Man, we can no longer talk in terms of defining a word. The only relevant word would be the proper name of the individual in question – and proper names do not have definitions in the usual sense. What we do here is identify those features possessed by the individual by virtue of which he counts as the individual he is. (This point is fairly close to the surface in the second and third paragraphs of Ch. 5 of Thomas's *Being and Essence*. See also Cajatan's Commentary on *Being and Essence*, Q. 7, secs. 64–5.) Thus to say that 'good', 'wise', etc., qualify the essence of the individual that is God is to say that this individual is good, wise, etc., and that if He were not good, wise, etc., He would not be the individual he is.

[2] This passage translated by Marcus Dods, New York, Random House (Modern Library Series), 1950, pp. 354–5.

[3] See, e.g., St. Anselm, *Monologium*, Ch. XVII.

[4] *God: His Knowability and Attributes*, ed. A. Preuss, St. Louis, Herder, 1941, p. 211. In his article 'Why is There Something Rather than Nothing?' (*Journal of Philosophy*, June, 1966) Fred Sommers attempts to identify some of the implications of holding that the attributes of God entail one another.

The Logical Status of 'God is Timeless'

For one thing, he argues that on this supposition, the Ontological Argument for the existence of God is sound.

[5] *The Ontological Argument*, ed. A. Plantinga; New York, Doubleday (Anchor Series), 1965, pp. 116–17.

[6] *Mind*, April, 1958, pp. 171–2.

[7] Ithaca, Cornell Press, 1960.

Martin says that traditional theologians such as St. Thomas and St. Anselm sometimes treat the term 'God' as a proper name. They also use it as a descriptive expression meaning 'the eternal, all-powerful, all-good creator of all things'. On Martin's view, when the term 'God' is used in this second way, the statement 'God is perfectly good' is a necessary truth and when the term 'God' is used as a proper name, 'God is perfectly good' is not a necessary truth. In this second case, Martin says, even though a given individual is perfectly good, we can conceive of that individual as other than perfectly good. Martin then argues that theologians such as St. Thomas and St. Anselm have been led to think that the individual whose name is 'God' could not fail to be perfectly good because they have been guilty of a mix-up regarding the syntactical status of 'God'. They have thought that because it would be inconsistent to say that the eternal, all-powerful, all-good creator of all things is other than perfectly good, it would also be inconsistent to say that the individual whose name is 'God' is other than perfectly good. Assume that 'God' is a proper name. Martin accounts for the fact that many theologians have regarded 'God is perfectly good' as a necessary truth, by suggesting that these theologians have confused the descriptive and proper-name occurrences of the term 'God'.

In the next section of this chapter, I address myself to the question of the syntactical status of the term 'God'. I there propose an analysis of this term designed to account for both the descriptive and proper-name uses mentioned by Martin. But it seems to me worth noting at this point, that the account Martin gives of the origins of the theological view he criticizes seems very implausible. Surely the idea that the individual named 'God' could not fail to be perfectly good is not the product of the simple-minded grammatical mix-up mentioned by Martin. It seems to me that the origin of this doctrine must be as I have described it above. It is ultimately grounded in the doctrine of essential predication as applied to the predicate 'perfectly good'.

[8] Pt. I, Ch. 58. This passage translated by M. Friedlander, New York, Hebrew Publishing Co., 1881; p. 211.

[9] *Ibid.*, Ch. 57, p. 206.

[10] Such an analysis is at least suggested by St. Thomas, *Summa Theologica*, Pt. I, Q. 13, A. 8. See also Father Norris Clarke's, 'On Professors Ziff, Niebuhr, and Tillich', *Religious Experience and Truth*, ed. S. Hook, New York University Press, 1961, p. 224; H. P. Owens's, 'The Evidence for Christian Theism', *Proceedings of the Aristotelian Society*, 1963, p. 124–5; and C. B. Martin's *Religious Belief*, Ch. 4.

¹¹ In an article entitled 'About "God" ' (*Religious Experience and Truth*, p. 195) Paul Ziff analyses the syntactical features of the term 'God' as it occurs in the sentence 'God exists'. He concludes that 'God' is a proper name. All of the grammatical features mentioned by Ziff characterize 'God' in 'God spoke to Moses' and 'God, have mercy on my soul'. They are all accounted for if 'God' is understood as a title-term rather than a proper name.

¹² 'On Professors Ziff, Niebuhr and Tillich', *Religious Experience and Truth*, pp. 224–5.

3

Timelessness and the Negative Predicates 'Immutable', 'Incorruptible' and 'Immortal'

> Genuine eternity (is that) by which God is unchangeable, without beginning or end; consequently, He is also incorruptible. For one and the same thing is therefore said, whether God is called eternal or immortal, or incorruptible, or unchangeable.

I quote from Bk. XV of St. Augustine's *Trinatate*.[1] In this chapter I want to explore Augustine's idea that we say the *same thing* about God whether we say that He is eternal, immortal, incorruptible or immutable.

I

(*a*) If an object changes, that object is different at a given time from what it was at an earlier time. This is what it is to change. Thus, in order to change, an object must exist at two moments in time. It follows that if an object is timeless (and thus lacks temporal position altogether) it does not change. The function, 'x is timeless' entails 'x is unchanging'.

Let us agree to a point assumed in the last chapter, *viz.*, that timelessness is an essential property of any individual possessing it. If a given individual is timeless, it would be logically impossible for that individual to exist at a given moment in time. It follows that it would be logically impossible for that individual to change. The function, 'x is (essentially) timeless' entails not only '*x* is unchang*ing*', but also '*x* is unchange*able*'.

To say that a given individual is *immutable* is to say that that individual cannot change. Now I think it must be acknowledged that there are a number of ways in which the predicate 'immutable' (or the phrase 'cannot change') might be understood. 'Cannot' in 'cannot change' might be given some kind of material import. An individual might count as immutable with respect to a given quality (e.g., goodness) if that individual were such that it would be psychologically, emotionally, etc., impossible for that individual to change as regards this feature. (I shall develop this point a little further in sec. II of Ch. 9.) But in the case before us, the predicate 'immutable' (or the phrase 'cannot change') must be analysed in terms of *logical* impossibility. If a given individual is timeless (and if timelessness is an essential property of any individual possessing it) then it is logically impossible for that individual to change. In a postscript to his discussion of the concept of eternity, Schleiermacher said that the notion of immutability is 'already contained in the idea of eternity'.[2] This is right, if 'eternity' means 'timeless' and if timelessness is an essential property of an individual possessing it. We should add that in this context, the modal element in the predicate 'immutable' (i.e., the element expressed in 'cannot' in the phrase 'cannot change') is here to be understood in its strongest possible sense.

I suggested in the last chapter that for most of the theologians of interest to us in this essay, the standard terms usually used to characterize God ('eternity', 'omnipotent', etc.,) attach to the title-term 'God' in such a way as to make propositions such as 'God is eternal', 'God is omnipotent', etc., necessary truths. The statement 'God is immutable' is a necessary truth. But as has just been pointed out, the term 'immutable' is a modal predicate. It has a modal element *within it* – quite independently of any semantical connection it may have with the title-term 'God'. Thus, 'God is immutable' has a *double modal* structure. Within the context of the present discussion, we can articulate this double modal structure with some precision. I'll approach this point in a series of easy logical steps:

The function 'x is timeless' entails the function 'x is immutable'. Thus, '(x) (If x is God, then x is timeless)' entails '(x) (If x is God, then x is immutable)'. Hence, 'N(x) (If x is God, then x is timeless)' entails 'N(x) (If x is God, then x is immutable)'. Given our analysis of the modal elements working *within* the predicates 'timeless' and 'immutable', we can conclude that 'N(x) (If x is God, then N$(x$ lacks temporal position and temporal extension))' entails 'N(x) (If x is God, then N$(x$ does not change))'. Of course, we already know how to read the first half of this latter formula. We analysed it rather closely at the end of the last chapter. Since the second half of the formula is entailed by the first half, we know how to read the second half too. The first 'N' in the second half records a semantical connection between the title-term 'God' and the predicate 'immutable'. The second 'N' registers the modal element within the predicate 'immutable'. With respect to the individual that is God (if there is one), to change in any way whatsoever would constitute a loss of identity. The second half of the formula thus tells us that it is a logical condition of bearing the title 'God' that an individual be *essentially* unchanging.

In Pt. I, Q. X, article two of the *Summa Theologica*, St. Thomas says: 'The notion of eternity follows immutability, as the notion of time follows movement, as appears from the preceding article'. I have suggested above that the function 'x is eternal (timeless)' entails 'x is immutable'. St. Thomas seems to be claiming the reverse, i.e., that 'x is immutable' entails 'x is eternal (timeless)'. The argument for Thomas's view given in *a*.1 (the 'preceding article') is as follows:[3]

> *I answer that,* Just as we attain to the knowledge of simple things by way of composite things, so we must reach to the knowledge of eternity by means of time, which is nothing but *the number of movement according to before and after*. For since succession occurs in every movement, and one part comes after another, the fact that we reckon before and after in movement makes us apprehend time,

which is nothing else but the number of before and after in movement. Now in a thing lacking movement, and which is always the same, there is no before and after. Just as therefore the nature of time consists in the numbering of before and after in movement, so likewise in the apprehension of the uniformity of what is absolutely outside of movement consists the nature of eternity.

This argument seems to me to be confusing and deficient. One thing that makes it confusing is that it contains a number of distinguishable themes. Let us agree that time is (in some sense) a function of motion. If there were no motion, there would be no time. Secondly, let us agree to two other claims advanced in this passage, *viz.*, that we measure time by motion (the sun, clocks, etc.) and that we apprehend time by apprehending motion. These are distinguishable theses as was pointed out by John Locke. (Locke agreed to the first but denied the second.)[4] The central claim made in Thomas's argument (the one referred to in *a*.2) is still to come; and so far as I can see, it derives no support from any of the three theses just mentioned. St. Thomas says: '... in a thing lacking movement, and which is always the same, there is no before and after'. I take it that this is the principle that supports the conclusion that '*x* is immutable' entails '*x* is eternal (timeless)'. But I cannot see that St. Thomas has given us any reason for supposing that a motionless (or changeless) being must be timeless. Even if time is (in some sense) a function of motion, a motionless being might be in time – time that is a function of the motion of *other* beings. In fact, so far as I can see, St. Thomas has not given us reason for supposing that a motionless being could not be assigned a specific and measurable duration. Even if time is measured by motion, a motionless being might have a measurable duration – a duration calculated by reference to the motion of *other* beings.

Shall we then reject the claim that '*x* is immutable' entails '*x* is eternal (timeless)'. I don't think we can do that just yet. Try the following argument in place of the one given by St. Thomas.

Timelessness—'Immutable', 'Incorruptible' and 'Immortal'

Assume for the moment that if a given individual has location in time, it would at least be consistent (though it might be false) to say that that individual persists for more than one moment. Further (and this is a second assumption) if it is consistent to say that a given individual persists for more than one moment in time, it is consistent (though, again, it might be false) to say that that individual undergoes change. Under these two assumptions, if a given individual is such that it is logically impossible for that individual to undergo change (i.e., if a given individual is immutable in the strong sense of 'immutable'), then that individual is such that it is logically impossible for it to exist for more than one moment in time (from the second assumption); and if a given individual is such that it is logically impossible for it to exist at more than one moment in time, then it is also such that it would be logically impossible for it to have location in time (from the first assumption). It follows that if an individual is immutable (in the strong sense of 'immutable'), that individual has no location in time. Since lack of temporal location entails lack of temporal extension, an individual that is immutable (in the strong sense) must be timeless. This argument rests on two assumptions concerning the sufficient conditions for certain *possibilities*: viz. (1) temporal location is a sufficient condition for the possibility of persistence; and (2) the possibility of persistence is a sufficient condition for the possibility of change. I offer these assumptions as plausible, but I shall not try to show that they are correct.

Let's take stock: I argued above that the function 'x is (essentially) timeless' entails the function 'x is immutable' where 'immutable' takes its strongest interpretation. This conclusion plus our internal analyses of the predicates 'timeless' and 'immutable' furnished the basis for the claim that 'N(x) (If x is God, then N(x lacks temporal position and temporal extension))' entails 'N(x) (If x is God, then N(x does not change))'. I then tried to supply an alternative to St. Thomas's argument for the claim that 'x is immutable' (in the strong sense) entails 'x is timeless'. If this second argument could be accepted, then by the same sequence of logical steps as was used above when working with the entailment in the other direction we could now conclude that 'N(x) (If x is God, then N(x does not change))' entails N(x) (If x is God, then N(x lacks temporal position and temporal extension))'. Adding everything together, we could draw the final conclusion so: 'N(x) (If x is God, then N(x lacks temporal position and temporal extension))' *entails and is entailed by* 'N(x) (If x is God, then N(x does not change))'.

(*b*) Focus now on the predicate 'incorruptible'. If an individual ceases to exist, that individual exists at one moment and does not exist at some later moment. This is what it is to cease to exist. Thus, as above, unless a being exists at some moment before a moment when it does not exist, it does not cease to exist. It follows that if an object is timeless (and thus lacks temporal position) it does not cease to exist. It follows, further, that if it is logically impossible for a given individual to occupy time, it is also logically impossible for that individual to cease to exist. The function 'x is (essentially) timeless' entails not only 'x *does not* cease to exist', it entails as well 'x *cannot* cease to exist' – where 'cannot' takes its strongest possible interpretation. If an individual is essentially timeless, it is logically impossible for that individual to cease to exist.

In the context of a technical theology, to say that a thing is *incorruptible* is to say that that thing cannot cease to exist. As in the case of the predicate 'immutable', the modal element involved in the predicate 'incorruptible' is subject to a number of interpretations. The 'cannot' in 'cannot cease to exist' might mean, e.g., that it is physically or causally impossible for the thing under discussion to cease to exist. (I shall return to this point in sec. II of Ch. 9 where I shall also say something about the possibility of assigning a material interpretation to 'cannot' in 'cannot change'.) But in the case before us, the 'cannot' in 'cannot cease to exist' must be given its strongest possible interpretation. If a given individual is essentially timeless, then it is *logically* impossible for that individual to cease to exist.

We have already reminded ourselves that statements of the form 'God is ϕ' – where 'ϕ' takes standard divine attributes as values – are necessary truths. Thus, 'God is incorruptible' is a necessary truth. But 'incorruptible', like 'immutable' is a modal predicate. It has a modal element within it whatever may be its semantical attachment to the title-term 'God'. Thus, like 'God is immutable', 'God is incorruptible' has a double modal structure. Again, in the present context, this structure can be elucidated with some precision. The function 'x is (essentially) timeless' entails 'x is incorruptible' (where 'incorruptible' takes its strongest sense). Following the logical steps used above when dealing with the predicate 'immutable', we can conclude that 'N(x) (If x is God, then N(x lacks temporal position and temporal extension))' entails 'N(x) (If x is God, then N(x does not cease to exist))'. The second half of the last formula is subject to the same sort of interpretation as was given above for the second half of the corresponding formula concerning the attribute of immutability. It is a necessary truth that if a given individual is God, any individual that goes out of existence could not (or could not have been) that individual. It is a logical condition of bearing the title 'God', that an individual be *essentially* stable.

Consider the following argument for the claim that if a given individual is incorruptible (in the strong sense of 'incorruptible'), that individual is timeless.

Assume that if a given individual has temporal extension (even if it is endless duration), it is consistent (though it might be false) to say that that individual ceases to exist. We may conclude that if a given individual is incorruptible (in the strong sense) that individual does not have temporal extension. But, by hypothesis, if a given individual has temporal position and no temporal extension (i.e., is a momentary being), that individual ceases to exist. It thus follows that if a given individual is incorruptible (in the strong sense), that individual lacks temporal extension and also lacks temporal position. The function '*x* is incorruptible' (in the strong sense), entails the function '*x* is timeless'.⁵

I have argued that the function '*x* is (essentially) timeless' entails the function '*x* is incorruptible' (in the strong sense). Together with our internal analysis of the predicates 'timeless' and 'incorruptible' this argument supplied the ground for the conclusion that 'N(*x*) (If *x* is God, then N(*x* lacks temporal position and temporal extension))' entails 'N(*x*) (If *x* is God, then N(*x* does not cease to exist))'. I have just suggested an argument for the claim that '*x* is incorruptible' (in the strong sense) entails '*x* is (essentially) timeless'. If this last argument could be accepted, the upshot would be that 'N(*x*) (If *x* is God, then N(*x* does not cease to exist))' entails 'N(*x*) (If *x* is God, then N(*x* lacks temporal position and temporal extension))'. The final conclusion would be that 'N(*x*) (If *x* is God, then N(*x* lacks temporal position and temporal extension))' *entails and is entailed by* 'N(*x*) (If *x* is God, then N(*x* does not cease to exist))'.

(*c*) In the passage quoted above from Augustine's *Trinatate* it was claimed that if an individual is eternal, that individual has no beginning in time. Now 'immutable' means 'cannot change' and 'incorruptible' means 'cannot cease to exist'. Neither of these terms means 'cannot begin'. It might be thought that if a given individual begins to exist that individual has changed. But this would be a mistake. To change is to be different at one time from that at an earlier time. A being that does not exist at the earlier time cannot be said to be *different* at a later time from what it was at the earlier time. Thus, let us employ a predicate that carries the pre-analytical import 'cannot begin to exist'. The term 'ingenerable' is sometimes used for the purpose. The following two arguments suggest a possible analysis of the logical relations between the predicate 'timeless' and the predicate 'ingenerable'.

If a given individual is essentially timeless, that individual is such that it would be logically impossible for that individual to exist at a given moment in time. Thus, if an individual is essentially timeless, it is logically impossible for that individual to begin to exist since to begin to exist requires (logically) that one exist at a moment in time posterior to a time when one did not exist. On the assumption that timelessness is an essential property of an individual possessing it, the function 'x is timeless' entails the function 'x is ingenerable' – where the modal element in the predicate 'ingenerable' takes its strongest interpretation.

Assume that if an individual has duration (even if its life extends indefinitely in the past), it is consistent (though it might be false) to say that that individual began to exist. Given this much, if an individual is such that it is logically impossible for that individual to begin to exist (i.e., is ingenerable in the strong sense), that individual does not have temporal extension. But, by hypothesis, a being having temporal location but no temporal extension (i.e., a momentary being) begins to exist. Thus, if it is logically impossible for a given individual to begin to exist, it follows that that individual lacks temporal location as well as temporal extension. The function 'x is ingenerable' (in the strong sense) entails 'x is (essentially) timeless'.

Following the pattern of argument used above with respect to both 'immutable' and 'incorruptible', if the function 'x is (essentially) timeless' entails and is entailed by the function 'x is ingenerable' (in the strong sense of 'ingenerable'), then '$N(x)$ (If x is God, then $N(x$ lacks temporal position and temporal extension))' entails and is entailed by '$N(x)$ (If x is God, then $N(x$ does not begin to exist))'. The second half of this formula makes clear the double modal structure of the statement 'God is ingenerable' – a structure it shares in common with both 'God is immutable' and 'God is incorruptible'.

(*d*) I turn, finally, to the predicate 'immortal'.

Kant claimed that if a given individual is corporeal (is a physical body), that individual must have extension in space. On Kant's view, there could be no such thing as a spatially extensionless body. This is probably right. It seems to me that the same can be said with respect to extension in time. If a given individual is corporeal, that individual has temporal, as well as spatial, extension. The same point holds as regards temporal position. A thing lacking position in time could not be a physical body. Thus, if we were presented with an individual that is timeless, we could conclude that that individual is not corporeal. Of necessity, timeless individuals are not physical objects.

Will this connection hold in reverse? I don't think so. A mind or an idea is probably not to be counted as a physical object – though it is probably to be counted as an object of some sort ('mind', 'idea', 'thought', 'feeling', etc., have the grammar of object-words and 'object' itself is very permissive). However, minds and ideas have both temporal extension and temporal location. 'x is timeless' does not seem to follow from 'x is incorporeal'.

Now, to say that some individual is *immortal* is to say, first, that that individual is alive and, secondly, that that individual will not cease to exist, i.e., will not cease to live, i.e., will not die.[6] By one of the arguments given above, if we knew that a given individual is (essentially) timeless, we could conclude that that individual is incorruptible (in the strong sense of 'incorruptible'); and from this we could derive the weaker claim that the individual in question will not cease to exist. If we then added a second piece of information, *viz.*, that the individual we are considering is alive, we might then have enough to conclude that the individual in question is immortal. However, it should be noticed that the reasoning we have just been through requires that we add 'x is alive' as a *second* datum. We could not have derived this from 'x is timeless'. It would thus appear that 'x is timeless' does not entail 'x is immortal' (since it does not entail 'x is alive') even if it does entail 'x is incorruptible' and thus 'x will not go out of existence'.

I could imagine a kind of Neo-Augustinian philosopher replying to this last observation as follows: The function 'x is timeless' entails the function 'x is incorporeal'. But, if a given individual is incorporeal, it must be a 'spiritual' object, i.e., it must be a soul. There are no other alternatives. This line of thinking presupposes what might be called a 'two substance' ontology. However, as Plato pointed out in the *Phaedo*, it is of the essence of a 'spiritual' object that it be alive: a 'spiritual' object could not cease to live and remain the object it is. Augustine seems to have held this view too.[7] Thus, if the function '*x* is timeless' entails the function '*x* is incorporeal', given the 'two substance' ontology, it also entails '*x* is alive'. If it is then true that '*x* is timeless' entails '*x* is incorruptible' and thus '*x* will not go out of existence', it would appear that we have all we need to conclude that '*x* is timeless' entails '*x* is immortal'.

One trouble with this Neo-Augustinian argument is that it rests too heavily on the 'two substance' ontology, i.e., on the claim that objects divide exhaustively into two groups, *viz.*, corporeal objects and 'spiritual' objects. Timeless objects are incorporeal. However, the number three is a model case of a timeless object. This is the sort of case we relied on when attempting to understand the idea of an object that exists, but does not exist in time. If this is right, then we surely must allow that there are incorporeal objects that are not 'spiritual' objects – at least, if it is of the essence of 'spiritual' objects to be alive. The number three is not alive. It thus seems to me that the above argument will not support the claim that '*x* is timeless' entails '*x* is alive' and hence will not support the claim that '*x* is timeless' entails '*x* is immortal'.

There is a sense, I think, in which the predicate 'immortal' does not really belong in the list of predicates we are discussing in this chapter. '*x* is timeless' does not seem to entail '*x* is immortal' because it does not seem to entail '*x* is alive'. Further, there would appear to be no plausible way of arguing that '*x* is immortal' entails '*x* is timeless'. An immortal being might have endless duration.[8] '*x* is timeless', and '*x* is immortal' seem to be logically independent. '*x* is immortal' should thus be distinguished from '*x* is immutable', '*x* is incorruptible', '*x* is ingenerable' and '*x* is

49

incorporeal', in that each of these others has at least some logical connection with '*x* is timeless'.

II

Let us assume that in the passage cited at the very beginning of this chapter, St. Augustine intended the term 'eternal' to mean 'timeless'. (This assumption squares well with the message conveyed in the passages cited from the *Confessions* in the first chapter of this essay. We shall see in the next chapter, however, that it does not fit well with what Augustine says when discussing the traditional problem of divine foreknowledge.) We have already seen (Ch. 2) that for Augustine, *all* divine attributes are essential to God's nature and thus that eternity (i.e., timelessness) must be regarded as an essential attribute of God. We are now in a position to draw two closely related conclusions:

(1) As understood by Augustine in the passage cited above, 'God is eternal (timeless)' entails 'God is immutable', 'God is incorruptible', 'God is ingenerable' and 'God is incorporeal'. If one were to ask for an interpretation of the modal elements involved in the first three of these implied predicates, we could answer with little hesitation. For example, the function '*x* is immutable' means: 'It is logically impossible for *x* to change'. With its full modal apparatus displayed, the statement 'God is immutable' means: 'Necessarily, the individual that is God (if there is one) is logically incapable of change'. This is an important clarificatory advance. The Augustinian understanding of the predicate 'eternal' provides the ground for analyses of other negative predicates usually assigned to God – analyses that include explications of the modal elements involved in these predicates. It does this by supplying the ground from which these latter predicates can be derived with precise interpretations of their modal elements fully explicit.

(2) There is at least some reason to think that each of the statements 'God is immutable', 'God is incorruptible', and 'God is ingenerable' (though not 'God is incorporeal')

Timelessness—'Immutable', 'Incorruptible' and 'Immortal'

entails 'God is eternal (timeless)'. I do not want to claim that any of the arguments used above when attempting to establish these reverse entailments are fully successful. Each of them involves one or more assumptions concerning the sufficient conditions of certain possibilities that I have not tried to defend. Still, the arguments in question are at least tempting; and if they could be accepted, we could now conclude that 'God is eternal (timeless)', 'God is immutable', 'God is incorruptible', and 'God is ingenerable' are *equivalent* statements since each entails and is entailed by a single statement, *viz.*, 'God is eternal (timeless)'. It would also follow that each of these statements entails 'God is incorporeal', since this latter is entailed by 'God is eternal (timeless)' and thus would have to be entailed by any statement that is logically equivalent to 'God is eternal (timeless)'.

It may be that this last point is what St. Augustine had in mind (or in the back of his mind) when he said that we say the *same thing* about God whether we say that He is eternal, immortal, incorruptible or immutable. If this is what he had in mind, then the point is not that each of these predicates has the same *meaning*. What Augustine was suggesting is that we get the same predication results regardless of where we begin in this cluster of ideas. Of course, I have tried to show that, as stated by Augustine, this claim is not entirely correct. 'Immortal' does not seem to fit into this cluster. But the point is surely instructive nonetheless. The predicate 'eternal', when interpreted to mean 'timeless', appears to have a number of more or less intimate logical relations to a wide range of the other negative predicates that are usually used to characterize God.

NOTES

[1] *The Trinity*, Bk. XV, Ch. 5, sec. 7. This passage translated by Stephen McKenna, Washington Catholic University Press (The Fathers of the Church Series), 1963, p. 459.

[2] *The Christian Faith*, postscript to para. no. 52.

[3] This passage taken from *The Basic Writings of St. Thomas*, ed. A. Pegis, pp. 74–5.

[4] See Bk. II, Ch. 14 of the *Essay Concerning Human Understanding*.

[5] A version of this argument occurs in Norman Malcolm's article, 'Anselm's Ontological Arguments'. See *The Ontological Argument*, ed. A. Plantinga, New York, Doubleday, 1965, p. 144.

[6] Note: 'Immortal' is not a modal predicate as is, e.g., 'immut*able*'. (See 'Soul: Immortality of', *Catholic Encyclopedia*, 1967.)

[7] See Augustine's *The Immortality of the Soul*, Chs. 1–6; and *Soliloquies* 2, 19, 33.

[8] A little reflection will show that an argument of the sort I used above when attempting to support the claim that 'x is immutable' entails 'x is timeless' could not be employed here. The trouble is that 'immortal' unlike 'immutable' is not a modal predicate.

4
Timelessness, Foreknowledge and Free Will[1]

In Pt. V, sec. III of the *Consolation of Philosophy*, Boethius said that if God is infallible and if God knows the outcome of human actions in advance of their performance, then no human action is voluntary. Further, Boethius held that at least some human actions are voluntary. It was thus incumbent upon him to deny either that God is infallible or that God knows how human beings will act prior to the time of action. Boethius opted for the second of these alternatives. He held that God is timeless. A timeless being cannot know the outcome of human actions in advance of their performance. To know something before it happens requires that one's cognitions be located in time relative to the thing in question. A timeless being could not have temporally located cognitions.

In this chapter, I shall examine the problem of divine foreknowledge and Boethius's solution to it. I want to be sure that we understand the doctrine of timelessness as it works in this context. This is one of the more important places in the history of Christian theology where the doctrine worked to the advantage of the systematic theologian. What we discover here could have an important bearing when we come to our final evaluation of the doctrine itself.

God and Timelessness

I

Historically, there have been any number of attempts to formulate the problem of divine foreknowledge. In what is to follow I shall work with a version of the problem that seems to me to be relatively elegant and that also seems to me to contain the essentials of the problems with which Boethius was concerned in the *Consolation*. As I read Boethius's discussion, the items generating the problem are two in number, *viz.*, (1) the claim that God is infallible, and (2) the claim that God knows the outcome of human actions in advance of their performance. Further, there seems to me to be six theses that must be distinguished before the interior of these two claims can be exposed. I shall refer to these six theses as the *assumptions* working in Boethius's formulation of the problem.

Assumption I: 'God is omniscient' is a necessary statement. Here, 'God' appears as a title-term and the proposition as a whole is to be read as having hypothetical form.

Assumption II: If an individual is omniscient, that individual believes all true propositions. This is part of the meaning of the predicate 'omniscient'. '$N(x)$ (P) (If x is omniscient, then if P, x believes that P).' In this formula, 'P' takes propositions as values. If two plus two equals four, then if x is omniscient, x believes that two plus two equals four.

Assumption III: If a given individual is omniscient, then that individual believes nothing that is false. This, too, is part of the meaning of the predicate 'omniscient'. Omniscient beings hold no false beliefs. (Assumption III does not follow from Assumption II. It is logically possible that an individual who believes all true propositions also believes a false proposition, i.e., the negation of one of the other propositions that he believes.)

A good many contemporary philosophers have held that a proper application of the verb 'knows' requires not only that the knower hold a true belief, but also that he have evidence or grounds for the belief in question. However,

Timelessness, Foreknowledge and Free Will

there are relatively clear cases in which the verb 'knows' applies even though the knower does not have evidence or grounds for his belief. Consider the crystal-ball gazer who 'sees' future events in his crystal. He gets it right every time; he makes no mistakes in ten thousand tries. Assume that the crystal-ball gazer is not permitted to know his own record. In this situation there is nothing that could be counted as grounds or evidence for his beliefs about the future. Still, if he got it right every time, I think we would have to admit that he *knows* what is going to happen in the future – though we might also have to admit that we do not understand how his knowing-device works. This kind of case is central to the present topic. John Calvin says:[2]

> When we attribute foreknowledge to God, we mean that all things have been and perpetually remain before his eyes, so that to his knowledge nothing is future or past, but all things are present; and present in such a manner, that he does not merely conceive of them from ideas formed in his mind, as things remembered by us appear to our minds, but he holds and sees them as if (*tanquam*) actually placed before him.

Boethius says precisely this same thing in Pt. V, sec. VI of the *Consolation*. He says that God's foreknowledge involves a kind of 'vision' of events and circumstances foreknown.[3] It is not based on evidence nor does it have anything that would count as grounds. Assumptions II and III together yield the conclusion: 'N(x) (P) (If x is omniscient, then if P, x believes that P and if x believes that P, then P)'. This seems to me to be enough to warrant the claim that if a given individual is omniscient, that individual *knows* all facts. This analysis excludes the idea that God's knowledge is based on evidence or grounds.

Assumption IV: Omniscience is an essential property of any individual possessing it. If a given individual is omniscient, that individual would not be the individual it is if it were not omniscient. A statement of the form 'If x is Yahweh, then x is omniscient' is a necessary truth, if it is true at all.

God and Timelessness

Boethius said that God 'cannot in anything be mistaken' (*nescia falli*).[4] I shall interpret this as follows: If a given individual is God, it is logically impossible that that individual should hold a false belief. The 'cannot' in 'cannot be mistaken' is here interpreted in its strongest possible sense. If Yahweh is God, then it is conceptually impossible for Yahweh to hold a false belief. Any individual holding a false belief could not be Yahweh: 'Yahweh is God' entails '"Yahweh believes P" entails "P" '. I shall refer to this as the doctrine of divine infallibility.

This interpretation of the notion of infallibility is a consequence of the assumptions made above. Assumptions I and IV together yield the conclusion: 'N(x) (If x is God, then N(x is omniscient))'. This tells us that it is a necessary condition of bearing the title 'God' that an individual be such that he could not fail to be omniscient. If we integrate Assumption III into this formula, the conclusion is this: 'N(x) (P) (If x is God, then N(If x believes P, then P))'. This affirms that it is a logically necessary condition of bearing the title 'God' that an individual be such that he could not hold a false belief.

Assumption V: If a given individual is God, that individual has always existed and will always exist. Let this be a necessary truth. The conclusion is that it is a logically necessary condition of bearing the title 'God' that an individual have duration extending indefinitely both forward and backward in time. (This is the assumption that Boethius will eventually deny.)

Assumption VI: If an individual exists at a given moment in time, then in order to count as omniscient, that individual must hold any belief he holds at that moment in time. 'N(x) (P) (T) (If x is omniscient and exists at T, then if x believes P, x believes P at T)'. Here 'T' takes times (e.g., ten o'clock on Monday) as values.

I think we now have enough to attempt a formulation of the problem underlying Boethius's concerns in Pt. V of the *Consolation*.

Last Saturday afternoon, Jones mowed his lawn. Let us

assume that the individual whose name is 'Yahweh' is, in fact, God. It follows that (let us say) eighty years prior to Saturday, Yahweh believed that Jones would mow his lawn on Saturday (Assumptions I, II, V and VI). But from this we can conclude that at the time of action (Saturday), Jones *was not able* – i.e., it was *not within Jones's power* – to refrain from mowing his lawn.[5] The upshot is that Jones's mowing his lawn on Saturday cannot be counted as a voluntary action. No action is voluntary if it is not within the power of the agent at the time of action to refrain from its performance. This is the thumbnail sketch of the problem Boethius develops. Let's see if we can get a little clearer about its details.

Begin with the setting as just described. Jones mows his lawn on Saturday and Yahweh (who is God) believes eighty years earlier that Jones mows his lawn on Saturday. Let us suppose that at the time of action it *was* within Jones's power to refrain from mowing the lawn. The most obvious conclusion would seem to be that at the time of action, Jones was able to perform an action (a refraining action) the performance of which would have rendered one of Yahweh's earlier beliefs false. But Yahweh is infallible (since He is, in fact, God), and if an individual is infallible, it is logically impossible that that individual holds a false belief. Thus, on Saturday, Jones was not able to act in such a way as to render false a belief held by Yahweh eighty years earlier. To suppose that he was would be to suppose that at the time of action, Jones was able to do something having a conceptually incoherent description, *viz.*, something that would render false a belief held by Yahweh who is infallible. Hence, given that Yahweh believed eighty years ago that Jones mows his lawn on Saturday (which by Assumptions II and VI follows from the claim that Jones mowed his lawn on Saturday plus the supposition that Yahweh is omniscient and existed eighty years ago), if we are to assign Jones the power on Saturday to refrain from mowing his lawn, we must not describe that power as the ability so to act as to render one of Yahweh's beliefs false.

God and Timelessness

How then might we describe such a power *vis-à-vis* Yahweh and His belief? So far as I can see, there are only two other alternatives. First, we might try describing it as the power so to act that Yahweh believed otherwise than He did eighty years earlier; and, secondly, we might try describing it as the power so to act that Yahweh (who by hypothesis existed eighty years ago) did not exist eighty years ago: This last would be the power so to act that any individual who believed eighty years ago that Jones would mow his lawn on Saturday (one of which was, by hypothesis, Yahweh) would have held a false belief and thus would not have been Yahweh. Yahweh is *essentially* omniscient. Any individual holding a false belief could not be omniscient and thus could not be Yahweh.

However, neither of these alternatives can be accepted. As regards the first, let us agree that *had* Jones actually refrained from mowing his lawn on Saturday, Yahweh *would have* believed otherwise than he did believe eighty years earlier. This follows from the fact that Yahweh is omniscient (and thus believes all true propositions) plus the assumption that if an omniscient being exists at a given moment (T1) and believes P, that individual believes P at that moment (T1) (Assumptions II and VI). But this observation takes no account of the *facts* working in the case before us. Jones did *in fact* mow his lawn on Saturday. Thus Yahweh did *in fact* believe eighty years earlier that Jones would mow his lawn on Saturday. On Saturday Jones did not have the power to perform an act the performance of which would require that Yahweh not have believed as He in fact believed eighty years earlier. By the time Saturday got here, Yahweh's belief was tucked away eighty years in the past. Nothing that Jones was able to do on Saturday could have had the slightest bearing on whether Yahweh held a certain belief eighty years earlier. For similar reasons, the last of the alternatives mentioned above cannot be accepted either. If Yahweh (a knowing person) existed eighty years earlier, we cannot assign Jones the power on Saturday to perform an act the description of which would

Timelessness, Foreknowledge and Free Will

entail that Yahweh did not exist eighty years earlier. Again, the fact that Yahweh existed eighty years prior to Saturday is a fact that is (as it were) 'over and done with', 'safely accomplished', etc., by the time Saturday got here. Nothing that Jones was able to do on Saturday could have had the slightest bearing on whether this fact was, indeed, a fact.

We are now ready for the conclusion: Given that Jones mowed his lawn on Saturday and given that Yahweh existed and was God eighty years prior to Saturday, it seems to follow (on the six assumptions made above) that Jones did not have the power on Saturday to refrain from mowing his lawn. The upshot is that Jones's mowing his lawn on Saturday cannot be counted as a voluntary action. Although I do not have an analysis of what it is for an action to be voluntary, it seems reasonable to suppose that a situation in which it would be wrong to assign Jones the *ability* or power to do *other* than he did, would be a situation in which it would also be wrong to speak of his action as voluntary.[6]

Since the argument just presented is somewhat complex, perhaps the following schematic representation may be of some use:

(1) 'Yahweh is omniscient and Yahweh exists at T_1' entails 'If Jones does A at T_2, then Yahweh believes at T_1 that Jones does A at T_2' (Assumptions II and VI).

(2) If Yahweh is (essentially) omniscient, then 'Yahweh believes P' entails 'P'. (The doctrine of divine infallibility from Assumptions III and IV.)

(3) It is not within one's power at a given time so to act that both 'P' and 'not-P' are true.

(4) It is not within one's power at a given time so to act that something believed by an individual at a time prior to the given time was not believed by that individual at the prior time.

(5) It is not within one's power at a given time so to act that an individual existing at a time prior to the given time did not exist at the prior time.

(6) If Yahweh believes at T_1 that Jones does A at T_2,

God and Timelessness

then if it is within Jones's power at T_2 to refrain from doing A then either: (1) It was within Jones's power at T_2 so to act that Yahweh believed P at T_1 and 'P' is false; or (2) it was within Jones's power at T_2 so to act that Yahweh did not believe as He did believe at T_2; or (3) it was within Jones's power at T_2 so to act that Yahweh did not exist at T_1.

(7) If Yahweh is (essentially) omniscient, then the first alternative in the consequent of line 6 is false (from lines 2 and 3).

(8) The second alternative in the consequent of line 6 is false (from line 4).

(9) The third alternative in the consequent of line 6 is false (from line 5).

(10) Therefore: If Yahweh is (essentially) omniscient and believes at T_1 that Jones does A at T_1, then it was not within Jones's power at T_2 to refrain from doing A (from lines 6 and 7–9).

(11) Therefore: If Yahweh is (essentially) omniscient and exists at T_1, then if Jones does A at T_2, it was not within Jones's power at T_2 to refrain from doing A (from lines 10 and 1).

In this argument, lines 1 and 2 are direct consequences of our initial assumptions – in particular, Assumptions II, III, IV and VI. Lines 3, 4 and 5 express what I take to be part of the concept of ability or power as it applies when speaking of human beings. Item 6 is offered as a necessary truth. If Yahweh believes at T_1 that Jones mows his lawn at T_2, then if Jones has the ability at T_2 to refrain from mowing his lawn, this power must be described in one of the ways listed in the consequent of 6. I do not know how to argue that these are the only alternatives, but I have been unable to think of another. Line 11, when generalized for all agents and actions and when taken together with what seems to be a minimum condition for the application of the phrase 'voluntary action', yields the conclusion that if Yahweh is (essentially) omniscient and exists at a given time (T_1), no human action performed after T1 is voluntary. Of course, nothing important in the argument turns on our selection of the name 'Yahweh' or on the selection of a particular time (T1, or eighty years ago) as a point of reference. By hypothesis, any individual that would qualify as the bearer of the title-term 'God' (whether his name be 'Yahweh' or 'Halifax') would be (essentially) omniscient and would exist at all moments in time (by Assumptions I and V). Since every human action is preceded by some moment in time, any individual that would count as God would exist and be (essentially) omniscient at a time prior to any given human action. This seems to be enough to warrant the conclusion: If God exists (i.e., if some individual bears the title 'God'), no human action is voluntary.

II

I now want to consider three attempts that have been made to deal with the problem of divine foreknowledge. Each of these attempts seems to me to be instructive though inadequate.

(*a*) Leibniz analysed the problem as follows:[7]

> They say that what is foreseen cannot fail to exist and they say so truly; but it follows not that what is foreseen is necessary. For necessary truth is that whereof the contrary is impossible or implies a contradiction. Now the truth which states that I shall write tomorrow is not of that nature, it is not necessary. Yet, supposing that God foresees it, it is necessary that it come to pass, that is, the consequent is necessary, namely that it exist, since it has been foreseen; for God is infallible. This is what is termed *hypothetical necessity*. But our concern is not this necessity; it is an absolute necessity that is required to be able to say that an action is necessary, that it is not contingent, that it is not the effect of free choice.

The statement 'Yahweh believes at T1 that Jones does A at T2' does not entail ' "Jones does A at T2" is necessary'. Leibniz is surely right about this. All that will follow from the first of these statements (given that Yahweh is God and is thus essentially omniscient) is that 'Jones does A at T2' is *true*, not that it is *necessarily true*. But this observation has no real bearing on the issue at hand. The following passage from St. Augustine's formulation of the problem may help to make this point clear.[8]

> Your trouble is this. You wonder how it can be that these two propositions are not contradictory and incompatible, namely that God has foreknowledge of all future events and that we sin voluntarily and not by necessity. For if, you say, God foreknows that a man will sin, he must necessarily sin. But if there is necessity there is no voluntary choice of sinning but rather fixed and unavoidable necessity.

In this passage the term 'necessity' (or the phrase 'by necessity') is used in contrast with the term 'voluntary' not (as in Leibniz) in contrast with the term 'contingent'. If one's action is necessary (or 'by necessity') this is to say that one's action is not voluntary. Augustine says that if the individual that is God has foreknowledge of human actions, the actions are necessary. But the form of this conditional is 'P implies Q' not 'P implies N(Q)'. 'Q' in the consequent of this conditional is the claim that human actions are not voluntary – that is, that one is not able, or does not have the power, to do other than he does.

Perhaps I can make this point clearer by reformulating the original problem in such a way as to make explicit the modal operators working within it. Let it be *contingently* true that Jones does A at T2. Let it be contingently true that Yahweh exists at T1 and, (again contingently) that Yahweh is God. It follows that Yahweh is essentially omniscient. It follows too that Yahweh believes at T1 that Jones does A at T2. This latter is a *contingent* statement. We can now conclude that it is *contingently* true that at T2 it is not within Jones's power to refrain from doing A. Had Jones been able (contingently) to refrain from doing A at T2, then either he was able (contingently) to perform an action that would have rendered one of Yahweh's beliefs false, or he was able (contingently) so to act that Yahweh did not

Timelessness, Foreknowledge and Free Will

hold the belief He held at T_1, or he was able (contingently) so to act that Yahweh did not exist at T_1. No one of these three alternatives can be accepted.

(b) In Bk. V, Ch. 9, sec. 2 of the *City of God*, St. Augustine reports Cicero's position on the problem of divine foreknowledge as follows:[9]

> What is it, then, that Cicero feared in the prescience of future things? Doubtless it was this – that if all things have been foreknown: and if they come to pass in this order, there is a certain order of things foreknown by God; and if a certain order of things, then a certain order of causes, for nothing can happen which is not preceded by some efficient cause. But if there is a certain order of causes according to which everything happens which does happen, then by fate, says he, all things happen which happen. But if this be so then there is nothing in our own power and there is no such thing as freedom of will; and if we grant this, says he, the whole economy of human life is subverted.

According to Augustine, Cicero could not face this conclusion. He thus reversed the order of the argument and drew the conclusion that God does not have foreknowledge of human actions:

> If there is free will, all things do not happen according to fate; if all things do not happen according to fate, there is not a certain order of causes, neither is there a certain order of things foreknown by God – for things cannot come to pass except they are preceded by efficient causes – but if there is no fixed and certain order of causes foreknown by God, all things cannot be said to happen according as He foreknew that they would happen. And further, if it is not true that all things happen just as they have been foreknown by Him, there is not, says he, in God foreknowledge of all future events.

On this account of the problem, God can know what will happen in the future only if future events (including human actions) are the products of 'a certain order of causes'. But if future events (including human actions) are the products of a 'certain order of causes', then no human action is voluntary. Here, the doctrine of divine foreknowledge enters the argument only as the ground of (i.e., the sufficient condition of) the claim that future events and actions are the products of a 'certain order of causes'. It is this latter thesis that does the heavy part in the reasoning: it is the one that entails determinism. Cicero's solution to the problem consists in denying that future events and actions are the products of a 'certain order of causes'. Given the pattern of Cicero's reasoning, this requires that he also deny that God has foreknowledge of the future.

The problem of divine foreknowledge formulated in the first section of this chapter makes no mention of the idea that human actions are the products of causes. We might suppose (for example, with St. Thomas[10]), that God's foreknowledge of human actions is, itself, the cause of those actions (though I'm not sure what this would mean). We might suppose, instead, that natural events and circumstances cause human actions. We might even hold, finally, that human actions have no causes. Let's agree that the whole idea of there being causes for human actions is absurd. But, Cicero (as interpreted by Augustine) would object that if human actions do not have causes, then God cannot have foreknowledge of them. That future events (including human actions) are products of a 'certain order of causes' is a necessary condition of God's foreknowledge of what will happen. Why should he agree to this? Perhaps what Cicero had in mind is that God can know what will happen in the future only if He knows the present state of the universe and only if there are (and He knows) certain rigid causal laws governing temporal events. Only then could God know what will happen in the future because only then could He have the grounds upon which to *predict* future events. But it seems to me that this line of thinking need not be endorsed. What reason is there for supposing that this is the only way that God could know what will happen in the future? As we have seen, Calvin and Boethius say that God foreknows things in that He 'sees them as if actually placed before him'. On this view, God does not *predict* the future on the basis of his knowledge of presently existing circumstances and causal laws. Like the crystal-ball gazer, God's foreknowledge is not the outcome of a prediction based on evidence. It is the result of a 'vision' involving nothing in the way of an inference or calculation. So far as I can see, Cicero does not address himself to the problem we are discussing. His 'solution' to the problem consists of denying a premise that is not involved in the issue. We can say (or fail to say) anything we choose about causes of human actions. If God is (essentially) omniscient and if God holds beliefs about the outcome of human actions in advance of their performance, then human actions are determined (i.e., not voluntary) whatever may be true about the causes (or lack thereof) involved in the situation.

(c) According to Arthur Prior, if God is omniscient and if God exists at a given time (e.g., T_1), He can know at T_1 only what is *true at that time* (e.g., at T_1). If a given proposition is not true at T_1, then even an omniscient being could not know it to be true at T_1. Prior then argues that with respect to a voluntary action occurring in the future relative to a given time (say, occurring at T_2), the claim that that action will be performed at T_2 is not true at T_1. This is so because the claim that the action will be performed at T_2 is neither true nor false at T_1. On Prior's account, the truth of 'Jones does A at T_2' is what theologians used to call 'indeterminate' at T_1. It follows, Prior says, that an omniscient being existing at T_1 could not know at T_1 that a voluntary action of a certain description will be performed at T_2. God does not have foreknowledge of human actions.[11]

I think it is interesting to note that Prior's analysis of, and solution to, the problem of divine foreknowledge is parallel in a number of respects to the analysis of and solution to this problem given by Cicero. Let me make this point clear.

Consider the following line of thinking. Suppose Jones mows his lawn on Saturday. It was then true eighty years ago that Jones would mow his lawn on Saturday. Hence, on Saturday, Jones was not able to refrain from mowing his lawn. To suppose that he was would be to suppose that on Saturday, Jones was able to act in such a way as to render false a proposition that was *already true* eighty years earlier. According to Prior, Peter de Rivo (fifteenth century), Cicero, Aquinas and Epicurus either used or discussed an argument of this sort when treating the topic of determinism. Such an argument was clearly anticipated in Ch. IX of Aristotle's *De Interpretatione*, and among contemporary writers it has been used with slight modification by Richard Taylor in his article 'Fatalism'.[12] This argument makes no mention of the causes of human actions. It turns, instead, on the notion of its being *true eighty years ago* that Jones mows his lawn on Saturday.

Now, Prior argues that in order for God to know at T_1 that Jones mows his lawn at T_2, it must be true at T_1 that Jones mows his lawn at T_2. Given the argument just sketched, if it is true at T_1 that Jones mows his lawn at T_2, then it is not within Jones's power at T_2 to refrain from mowing his lawn. If we put these two arguments together it will follow that the doctrine of divine foreknowledge entails determinism. It does so by way of an intermediate thesis, specifically, the claim that propositions describing human actions are true at times prior to the times that the actions are performed. This last thesis is the presupposition of God's foreknowledge – and it is this thesis that entails determinism. It is at this point that the argument before us can be seen to have a distinct similarity to Cicero's formulation of the problem. Cicero, too, made use of an intermediate thesis as the presupposition of divine foreknowledge (*viz.*, that human actions are products of 'certain order of causes'); and in both cases it is the intermediate thesis that delivers the final conclusion. Prior's solution to the problem of foreknowledge also follows the pattern of reasoning used by Cicero. In both cases, the solution consists of denying the intermediate thesis (the one that entails determinism and which is presupposed by the doctrine of divine foreknowledge) and then concluding that God does not have foreknowledge of human actions. Referring back to the

Timelessness, Foreknowledge and Free Will

scheme presented at the end of the first section of this chapter, both Cicero and Prior solve the problem by denying line 1. Line 1 reads:

> 'Yahweh is omniscient and Yahweh exists at T_1' entails 'If Jones does A at T_2, then Yahweh believes at T_1 that Jones does A at T_2'.

How can God be omniscient if He does not know the outcome of human actions in advance of their performance? An omniscient being must know everything. I think that both Cicero and Prior would answer this question as follows: An omniscient being must know everything that is *knowable*. But the fact that a man acts in a certain way at a certain time is not knowable prior to the time of action. No one could know it: the presupposition of foreknowledge is absent. Thus, God is omniscient though He does not know at T_1 that Jones mows his lawn at T_2.[18] For Cicero, this is so because Jones's action at T_2 is not the product of a 'certain order of causes' and for Prior, this is so because 'Jones mows his lawn at T_2' is not true at T_1. For both Cicero and Prior, that Jones mows his lawn at T_2 could not be known at T_1 by God or by anyone else. (I shall offer a critique of this thesis in note 28 of this chapter.)

I turn now to a critical examination of Prior's position. Clearly the centre of the matter concerns what Prior has to say about propositions of the form 'It is true at T_1 that Jones does A at T_2'.

Suppose I say: 'It is cold.' You reply: 'That was true yesterday, but it is not true today.' Your reply is intelligible. What it means is that it was cold yesterday, but it is not cold today. It is exactly as if you had replied: 'That is true in Alaska, but it is not true in California.' What this would mean is that it is cold in Alaska, but it is not cold in California. In these cases, a statement in which the *truth* of the original statement is assigned a date (or a special location) is translatable into a statement in which a *weather condition* is assigned a date (or a special location). A statement of the form ' "P" is true at T' (or ' "P" is true at S') is here restatable as a statement of the form ' "P at T" is true' (or ' "P at S" is true').

Now suppose I utter a statement of the form: 'Jones does A at T2'. You reply with a statement of the form: 'That is true at T1'. What would this mean? Surely it could not mean that at T1 Jones does A at T2. That would be nonsense. The problem here is that the action (A) mentioned in the original statement is dated *in the original statement*. If one then dates the truth value of the statement as a whole, it cannot be restated in accordance with the pattern just outlined. The resulting statement would then assign two (incompatible) dates to the action mentioned. We would get precisely the same kind of nonsense had we assigned a special position to the truth-value of a proposition in which it was claimed that Jones does A at some particular place in space.

How then shall we understand a statement of the form 'It is true at T1 that Jones does A at T2'?

Gilbert Ryle has suggested that a statement of this form should be understood as affirming that if one guessed, asserted, thought, etc., at T1 that Jones does A at T2, his guess, assertion, thought, etc., would have been right.[14] But Prior says that it was *not true* at T1 that Jones does A at T2. Surely Prior would be wrong if we were to accept Ryle's interpretation of 'It is true at T1 that Jones does A at T2'? We are assuming that Jones does A at T2. Thus if one had guessed, asserted, thought, etc., at T1 that Jones does A at T2, one would have been right. It might be that Prior has some other understanding of what it would be for it to be true at T1 that Jones does A at T2.

According to Richard Gale, a statement of the form 'It was true at T1 that Jones does A at T2', is to be read as affirming that at T1 there was sufficient evidence or grounds upon which to base a well-reasoned prediction that Jones does A at T2.[15] But Prior says that in order for one to know at T1 that Jones does A, it must be true at T1 that Jones does A at T2. I don't think Prior could defend this requirement if we were to accept Gale's reading of the statement 'It is true at T_1 that Jones does A at T_2'. On this reading Prior would be saying that God could know at T_1 that Jones does A at T_2 only if there were sufficient evidence at T_1 upon which to base a well-reasoned prediction that Jones does A at T_2. We have already seen that when dealing with God's foreknowledge (as in the case of the crystal-ball gazer) knowledge does not presuppose evidence of grounds. Thus, given Gale's suggestion as to the meaning of statements in which a date is assigned to the truth of 'Jones does A at T_2', I can see no reason for insisting that 'Jones does A at T_2' must be true at T_1 if God is to know at T_1 that Jones does A at T_2. To insist on this would be to disregard the special 'visionary' nature of God's foreknowledge. Again, it must be that Prior has some other understanding of statements in which the truth-value of 'Jones does A at T_2' is assigned a date prior to T_2.

Let's look at what Prior has to say on this matter. He writes:[16]

> What I want to say... is that nothing can be said to be truly 'going-to-happen' (*futurum*) until it is so 'present in its causes' as to be beyond stopping; until that happens, neither 'It will be the case that P' nor 'It will be the case that not P' is strictly speaking true.

With respect to Jones and his action at T_2, Prior would say that that action was not 'present in its causes' (and thus 'beyond stopping') at T_1. It is thus not true at T_1 that Jones does A at T_2. It would appear that we have here reverted to Cicero's version of, and solution to, the problem of divine foreknowledge. Prior's understanding of the issue is no longer just *similar* to Cicero's, it looks now to be precisely the same. In order for God to know at T_1 that Jones does A at T_2, it must be true at T_1 that Jones does A at T_2, i.e., Jones's action at T_2 must be 'present in its causes' at T_1. The claim that it is true at T_1 that Jones does A at T_2 is here replaced with (or perhaps reduced to) the claim that the causes of Jones's action are present at T_1. The deterministic conclusion flows from the causal thesis. Further, Prior's solution to the problem now appears to be precisely the solution offered by Cicero. It is not true at T_1 that Jones does A at T_2, i.e., Jones's action at T_2 is not 'present in its causes' at T_2. If this is an accurate account of what Prior has in mind, then I think he has erred in precisely the way Cicero erred. So far as I can see, the problem with which we are dealing requires nothing in the way of a comment about the causes of Jones's action. This 'solution' to the problem consists of denying a premise that is not part of the issue. The problem is exactly the same whether or not we say that Jones's action at T_2 is 'present in its causes' at T_1.

In another passage, Prior offers what seems to me to be quite a different account of the matter. He writes:[17]

> I can by my free choice, not exercised until tomorrow, cause a person's *guess*, made yesterday, to have been a correct one (I do this by simply deciding to do what he guessed I would do); and I can by the same free act convey the same retrospective verification to another person's guess, made right now, that the first person's guess *was* a correct one. It is so to speak still open to this latter guess, despite its past-tense subject matter, either to turn out to have been correct or to turn out not to have been correct; its present correctness, if it does turn out to be correct, is thus entirely contingent. But while contingent future and contingent future-infected pasts, can in this way be correctly or incorrectly guessed, I cannot see in what way that can be 'known', or, to put it another way, I cannot see in what way the alleged knowledge, even if it were God's, could be more than correct guessing. For there would be *ex hypothesi*, nothing that could *make* it knowledge, no present *ground* for the guess's correctness which a specially penetrating person might perceive.

The finished argument would appear to be as follows: God can know at T_1 that Jones does A at T_2 only if it is true at T_1 that Jones does A at T_2. However (and this by way of an analysis of this last remark), it is true at T_1 that Jones does A at T_2, only if there are sufficient *grounds* at T_1 upon which to base a well-reasoned prediction that Jones does A at T_2. This is precisely the interpretation given by Gale of propositions having the form 'It is true at T_1 that Jones

Timelessness, Foreknowledge and Free Will

does A at T2'. Prior then concludes that because there is not sufficient evidence or grounds at T1 to support a well-reasoned prediction, that it is then not true at T1 that Jones does A at T2. It follows that God cannot be said to *know* (as opposed to having guessed) at T1 that Jones does A at T2. If this is the view that Prior is advancing, then I think we must reply as we did when considering Gale's interpretation of statements in which the truth-value of a proposition is given a temporal location prior to the event mentioned in the proposition itself. Given Gale's interpretation of such statements, there appears to be no reason to suppose that 'Jones does A at T2' must be true at T1 in order for God to know at T1 that Jones does A at T2.

What then shall we say about whether it is true at T1 that Jones does A at T2? I am inclined to think that the whole idea of dating the truth-value of a statement in which a date is already assigned to a given event or action, is obscuristic and strange.[18] Further, I do not see that the problem we are discussing in this chapter requires that we proceed in this way. Jones does A at T2. This statement is true. We need not add that this statement is true, or false or 'indeterminate' *at T1*. 'Jones does A at T2' *is true*: that's quite enough to say. Of course, if 'Jones does A at T2' is true, then it must be known (infallibly believed) at T1 by an omniscient being. This is not to say that it is *true at T1* – it means only that it is *believed* (or known) *at T1*.

However, this last point is not of crucial importance as regards our final evaluation of Prior's position on this topic. If Prior thinks there is some advantage in formulating the problem of divine foreknowledge utilizing temporal qualifiers on the truth-values of the propositions that God believes, this procedure is likely to cause confusion, but I can see no other serious objection to it. We must ask only that Prior make clear to us what he means when he says that God's foreknowledge of human actions presupposes the *prior truth* of propositions describing these actions. Under one interpretation of this idea (*viz.*, Ryle's), 'It is true at T1 that Jones does A at T2' is trivially true if Jones does A at

T2. Prior would surely not deny it. On either of the two interpretations of this idea employed by Prior (Gale's interpretation and Prior's Cicero-like interpretation) Prior might be right in denying that it is true at T1 that Jones does A at T2. But on neither of these interpretations is there any reason for thinking that God's foreknowledge of Jones's action presupposes the prior truth of 'Jones does A at T2'. It thus seems to me that Prior's formulation of the problem of divine foreknowledge involves an obscure thesis which, when finally straightened out is either *trivially true* (and thus of no real interest) or *irrelevant* to the problem we are discussing in this chapter. Prior's 'solution' to the problem consists of denying this trivially true or irrelevant thesis. His solution (like the solutions given by Cicero and Leibniz) does not touch the problem with which we have been working in this discussion.

III

I now want to consider Boethius's solution to the problem of divine foreknowledge. I shall first explain what I take to be the central point of Boethius's thinking and then I shall attempt to compare Boethius's attack on the problem with the attack that is implicit in St. Augustine's treatment of this topic. I think that this comparison will help to clarify Boethius's idea.

(*a*) Let's start by supposing a situation in which God believes that Jones does A at T2, but one in which God's belief is located in time *after* Jones's action at T2. God believes at T3 that Jones does A at T2. Does Jones have the power at T2 to refrain from doing A? Of course, Jones does not have the power at T2 so to act that God will hold a false belief at T3. The individual that is God is infallible. This much is as it was before. But I think we would allow that at T2, Jones has the power to perform an act the performance of which would require that Yahweh not believe as He will, in fact, believe at T3. All we need add is that this power is one that Jones does not exercise. Note that the counterpart of this alternative in the situation where God's belief was located temporally *prior* to Jones's action, was not open to us. In this latter case we could not allow that Jones had the power at T2 to perform an act the performance of which would require that God would not have believed as He *did in fact* believe at T1. We feel no hesitation about assigning Jones the power at T2 to act in such a way as to alter the fact that God will hold a certain belief in the future relative to the time of action. But it would conflict with our ordinary understanding of what is and what is not within one's power to assign Jones the power at T2 to act in such a way as to alter the fact that God held a certain belief in the past relative to the time of action.

Now let's change the case. God believes that Jones does A at T2 and God holds this belief *at the time* that the action is being performed, i.e., at T2. Suppose God believes at T2 that Jones does A at T2 and suppose that God holds this belief at that time because he 'sees' Jones doing A at T2. We would allow that it is within Jones's power at T2 to refrain from doing A. In this case we would say that Jones has the power at T2 to perform an action (a refraining action) the performance of which would require that God 'see' and thus believe something other than what He in fact 'sees' and thus believes. (In terms of the schema given at the end of section I, it is a suitably modified version of line 4 that is being denied both in this case and in the case in which God holds His belief in the future relative to Jones's action at T2.)

Boethius denied that God has temporal extension. It is reasonable to suppose that he also denied that God has temporal position. Thus Assumption V in the list of original assumptions is to be rejected. God's (infallible) beliefs cannot be dated nor can they be located in time relative to human actions. The following passage is taken from St. Augustine's *City of God*. It sketches the picture of God and His cognitions that is clearly operating in Boethius's thinking.[19]

God and Timelessness

It is not as if the knowledge of God were of various kinds, knowing in different ways things which as yet are not, things which are, and things which have been. For not in our fashion does He look forward to what is future, nor at what is present, nor back upon what is past; but in a manner quite different and profoundly remote from our way of thinking. For He does not pass from this to that by transition of thought, but beholds things with absolute unchangeableness, so that of those things which emerge in time, the future, indeed, are not yet, and the present are now, and the past no longer are; but all of these are by Him comprehended in His stable and eternal presence. Neither does He see in one fashion by the eye, and another by the mind, for He is not composed of mind and body; nor does His present knowledge differ from that which it ever was or shall be, for those variations of time, past, present and future, though they alter our knowledge, do not affect His, 'with whom is no variableness, neither shadow of turning'. Neither is there any growth from thought to thought in the conception of Him in whose spiritual vision all things which He knows are at once embraced.

For Boethius (and for Augustine) God knows (infallibly believes) that Jones does A at T_2. God 'sees' or 'beholds' this action. God has what Augustine describes in this passage as 'spiritual vision' by which 'all things which He knows are at once embraced'. But we cannot go on to say that God knows what He knows at T_1 or at T_2 or at T_3; nor can we say that God knows what He knows *prior* to Jones's action, *at the time* that Jones is acting or *after* the time that Jones performs. God does not 'look forward to what is future, nor at what is present, nor back to what is past'. Given this set of restrictions, all we can say is that God *knows* (i.e., infallibly believes) that Jones does A at T_2. The verb 'knows' as well as 'sees' and 'beholds' must be used in the present tense only and must occur without time qualifiers such as 'T_2', or time-relative predicates such as 'before Jones does A'. Of course, these restrictions fit well with one of the major points made in the first chapter of this essay: a-temporal existence requires radical present tense description. The upshot seems to be that the only permissible description of God's knowledge of Jones's action is one that would be verbally identical to the one we would use if we were trying to describe *at T2* knowledge someone had *at T2* of an action going on *at T2*. The form of words required here is exactly the form we would use if we wanted to say that God *now* sees, and thus now believes something about, an action that is *now* in progress. Boethius is counting on us to conclude that the case before us is similar (as regards determinism) to the *second* of the cases considered above. He writes:[20]

> 'For doth thy sight impose any necessity upon these things which thou seest present?' 'No.' 'But the present instance of men may well be compared to that of God in this: that as you see some things in your temporal present, so He beholdeth all things in His eternal present.'

Boethius does *not* say that God 'sees' Jones's acting *at the time of action*. What he does say, however, is that the case in which God 'beholds' Jones's action timelessly (i.e., in 'His eternal-present')[21] is *comparable* to the case in which one sees Jones acting at the time of action. We are thus invited to conclude that Jones has the power at T2 to refrain from doing A. It is the power at T2 to perform an action (a refraining action) the performance of which would require that God 'see' and thus believe something other than what He in fact 'sees' and thus believes. Of course, by hypothesis, this power is one that Jones does not exercise.

If we can assume that the notion of a timeless knower is intelligible (an assumption I shall examine in Ch. 7 of this essay), I think that this reasoning is successful. So far as I can see, there is no way of formulating the problem of divine foreknowledge that does not involve locating God's cognitions in the *past* relative to the actions cognized.

Boethius's solution to (or dissolution of) the problem of divine foreknowledge entails a denial of the claim that God has *fore*knowledge of events and circumstances making up the temporal matrix. Boethius is quite explicit on this point. He says:[22]

> So that, if thou wilt weigh His knowledge with which He discerneth all things, thou wilt more rightly esteem it to be the knowledge of a never fading instant rather than a foreknowledge as of a thing to come. For which cause it is not called prescience or foresight, but rather providence, because placed far from inferior things, it overlooketh all things, as it were, from the highest top of things.

I shall comment further on this implication of Boethius's thinking in Ch. 9 of this essay. I mention it here only because it is one of the immediate consequences of Boethius's position that will be of interest to us later.

(*b*) In Bk. III of *De Libero Arbitrio*, St. Augustine writes:[23]

> Unless I am mistaken, you would not directly compel a man to sin, though you knew beforehand that he was going to sin. Nor does your prescience in itself compel him to sin even though he was certainly going to sin, as we must assume if you have real prescience. So there is no contradiction here. Simply you know beforehand what another is going to do with his own free will. Similarly, God compels no man to sin though he sees beforehand those who are going to sin by their own free will.

There are two comments of special interest in this passage. First, Augustine says that God's foreknowledge and, e.g., *my* foreknowledge of your actions are parallel as regards deterministic implications. Since my foreknowledge of your actions does not entail that your actions are determined, God's foreknowledge of your actions does not entail determinism either. Schleiermacher made precisely this same point in para. 55 of *The Christian Faith*. He said:[24]

> In the same way, we estimate the intimacy between two persons by the foreknowledge one has of the actions of the other, without supposing that in either case, the one or the other's freedom is thereby endangered. So even the divine foreknowledge cannot endanger freedom.

Secondly, Augustine says that with respect to my foreknowledge of your actions, what I know before you act is what you are going to do 'with your own free will'. The same

Timelessness, Foreknowledge and Free Will

is true with respect to God's foreknowledge of your action. Augustine develops this point in considerable detail in Bk. V of the *City of God*;[25] and the same idea has been expanded and utilized by a number of other traditional as well as contemporary Christian theologians. In the *Concordia Libitrii*, for example, Luis De Molina writes as follows:[26]

> It is not that since He [God] foreknew what would happen from these things which depend on the created will that it would happen; but, on the contrary, it was because such things would happen through the freedom of the will that He foreknew it; and that He would foreknow the opposite if the opposite was to happen.

The point seems to be that God knows in advance that a given person is going to *choose* to perform a certain action at some specific time in the future. With respect to the case of Jones, not only does God know at T1 that Jones does A at T2, He also knows at T1 that this action will be performed *freely*. In the words of Emil Brunner, 'God knows that which will take place in freedom in the future as something which happens in freedom.'[27] What God knows at T1 is that Jones *freely* does A at T2.

I think that most of us would agree that when dealing with ordinary human agents, it is perfectly possible to know how another is going to act in advance of the action. I think we would all agree that Augustine, De Molina and Brunner are right in thinking that we can sometimes know what another is going to do 'with his own free will'. When my wife is in the throes of decision as to which of two kinds of pie to buy for supper, I know how she is going to choose. There is only one kind of pie we like: she always buys apple. But, surely, my wife chooses apple of her own free will. The fact that I know how she will choose before the decision is made does nothing to diminish this fact.[28] It follows, I think that if God's foreknowledge of human actions has the same implications for determinism as does the foreknowledge an intimate friend can have of another's action (as Augustine and Schleiermacher maintain) then God can have foreknowledge of how another will *freely choose* to act.

Now, on the set of assumptions itemized in the first section of this chapter, the claim that God knows in advance how another will act *with his own free will*, is incoherent. If God knows (infallibly believes) at T_1 that Jones does A at T_2, it follows that Jones is not able at T_2 to do other than A at T_2 (for reasons already given). Thus, if God knows (infallibly believes) at T_1 that Jones does A at T_2, it follows that Jones does A at T_2, but *not freely*. If God believed at T_1 that Jones does A at T_2, it follows that Jones's action at T_2 is not free; and if God *also* believed at T_2 that Jones acts freely at T_2, it would follow that God holds a false belief — which is absurd. What this shows, is that the analysis we have given of divine foreknowledge, is not parallel to the analysis one would have to give of the knowledge an ordinary human being might have of another's future action. On our account, God's foreknowledge must differ from ordinary human foreknowledge, because the first entails determinism and the second does not. If we can put our finger on the precise source of this difference, we shall be able to say exactly where St. Augustine would object to the analysis we have given of divine foreknowledge. St. Augustine would say that we shall not have it right until we have exhibited the case of divine foreknowledge as parallel to the case of human foreknowledge and until we have exhibited both as free of deterministic implications.

Let's look at a case of ordinary human foreknowledge of another's action.

Smith is an ordinary man and an intimate friend of Jones. Let's suppose that Smith believes at T_1 that Jones does A at T_2. We make no assumptions concerning the truth or falsity of Smith's belief. We assume only that he holds it. Given only this much, it would be reasonable to say that it was within Jones's power at T_2 to do something (*viz.*, A) that would render the belief held by Smith true; and it would also be reasonable to say that it was within Jones's power at T_2 to do something (*viz.*, not-A) that would render Jones's belief false. So much seems apparent.

Now let's suppose that Smith *knew* at T_1 that Jones does

Timelessness, Foreknowledge and Free Will

A at T2. In order to keep the case in line with our discussion of God's foreknowledge, let us suppose that Smith is a very special knower — a crystal-ball gazer who always gets it right. Within this context, to say that Smith knows at T1 that Jones does A at T2 is simply to say that Smith correctly believes at T1 that Jones does A at T2. It follows, of course, that Jones *does* A at T2. If he did not, we could not say that Smith knew (i.e., *correctly* believed) at T1 that Jones does A at T2. But now let's inquire about what Jones was *able to do* at T2. I see no reason to deny that it was within Jones's power at T2 to refrain from doing A — understanding this to be the power at T2 so to act that the belief held by Smith at T1 was false. If we suppose that Smith *knew* at T1 that Jones does A at T2, what we are supposing is that Smith believed at T1 that Jones does A at T2 and, *as an additional contingent fact*, that the belief held by Smith at T1 was true. What appears to be a single contingency, *viz.*, the fact that Smith *knew* something at T1, really involves two contingencies, *viz.*, the fact that Smith held a certain belief at T1 and, secondly, the fact that that belief is true. When we raise the question of what Jones is able to do at T2, we must agree, of course, that it was not within Jones's power at T2 so to act that Smith did not believe as he did at T1. But, as regards the *second* contingency involved in Smith's knowledge (i.e., the fact that the belief is true) there appears to be no reason why we might not assign Jones the power at T2 to act in such a way that this second contingency fails. Paradoxical though it may seem (and it seems paradoxical only for a moment) Jones can be assigned the power at T1 so to act that what was in fact knowledge at T1 was not knowledge but false belief. This is simply to say that Jones can be assigned the power at T2 so to act that the belief held by Smith at T1 (which was in fact true) was (instead) false. We are required only to add that since Smith's belief was, *in fact*, true (i.e., was, *in fact*, knowledge) Jones did not, *in fact*, exercise this power. If Smith believes at T1 that Jones does A at T2, then as long as Jones does not exercise the power he has at T2 to refrain from doing A, Smith may be described as having *known* (correctly believed) at T1 that Jones does A at T2. (In terms of the schema given at the end of section I, it is again a modified version of line 4 – with 'known' in for 'believed' – that is here being denied.)

Now let's consider the case of divine foreknowledge as described in the first section of this chapter. Let us suppose that God knows at T1 that Jones does A at T2. As in the case of Smith's foreknowledge, we can again conclude that Jones *does* A at T2. Had Jones failed to do A at T2, God could not be described as having known at T1 that Jones would do A at T2. So far, the parallel with Smith's foreknowledge is secure. But now let's inquire about what Jones is *able to do* at T2. Again, following the Smith case we cannot describe Jones as having the power to refrain from doing A – understanding this to be the power so to act that God did not believe as He in fact believed at T1. But, unlike the Smith case, we also cannot assign Jones the power to refrain from doing A – understanding this to be the power so to act that the belief held by God at T1 was *false*. Here is the difference that makes the difference. If we assume that God held a certain belief at T1, it is not *an additional contingent fact* that this belief is true. Unlike Smith, the individual that is God is *infallible*. On the analysis we have given of this notion, to say that a given individual, e.g., Yahweh, is infallible is to say that 'Yahweh believes P' *entails* 'P'. The consequence is that while we could identify *two* contingencies involved in the case of Smith's knowledge of Jones's future action, we can identify only one contingency involved in God's foreknowledge of that action – *viz.*, the fact that God holds a certain belief at T1. Thus, while we could assign Jones the (unexercised) power at T2 to act in such a way as to render Smith's true belief false (i.e., to reverse the second contingency involved in Smith's knowledge) no such power can be assigned in the case of God's foreknowledge. There is no *second* contingency that could be reversed. 'Yahweh believes P' *entails* ' "P" is true'.

We can now see where St. Augustine would have to

object to the analysis we have given of divine foreknowledge. Since Augustine holds that God's foreknowledge of human actions is parallel in relevant respects to ordinary human foreknowledge of human actions (except, perhaps, that in the everyday case of human foreknowledge, the belief is supported by evidence, while St. Augustine, like Calvin and Boethius would say that in the case of God beliefs do not rest on evidence), he must deny that God is *infallible* in the sense indicated above. As we have just seen, this is the crucial point of difference between Smith's foreknowledge and God's foreknowledge. This is the difference that yields the variation as regards determinism in the two cases.

Would St. Augustine deny that God is infallible? Surely not. But it seems to me that St. Augustine could readily deny that God is infallible *in the sense* of 'infallible' given above. After all, the notion with which we have been working in this chapter is not the ordinary notion of infallibility. If I say that I have an infallible method of predicting the weather, I do not mean that it would be *logically* impossible for that method to fail. If I say that Hannibal had infallible military judgement, I do not mean that it was *logically* impossible for Hannibal to make a mistake in matters of this sort. It is not clear to me how the ordinary notion of infallibility should be analysed, but what does seem clear is that the analysis we have been using in this discussion is much too strong to serve. St. Augustine might well deny that God is infallible in the strong sense we have specified. If he did, I think that he would have the facts of ordinary discourse firmly on his side.

This brings me to the final and central point I want to make in this connection. The notion of an infallibility specified at the beginning of this chapter was a direct consequence of our analysis of the notion of omniscience (Assumptions II and III, more specifically, Assumption III) plus our assumption that omniscience is an *essential* property of any individual possessing it (Assumption IV). The analysis of the notion of omniscience offered in Assumptions II and III seems to me to be unexceptionable. No

Christian theologian would deny it. It thus seems to me that implicit in the claim that divine foreknowledge is parallel to human foreknowledge (a parallel insisted on by Augustine, Schleiermacher, De Molina and Brunner) is a denial of the idea that omniscience is an essential property of any individual possessing it. The centre of Augustine's remark on the topic of divine foreknowledge seems to me to commit him to a denial of Assumption IV.

Let us suppose that Yahweh is omniscient. We then know that Yahweh holds no false beliefs. But shall we then go on to say that the consequence of holding a false belief would be that Yahweh would not be the individual He is? Is the predicate 'omniscient' so related to the concept of *being* (or same being) that an omniscient being would not be the individual he is if he were not omniscient?

Suppose that we knew of an individual who knows everything and who holds no false beliefs. Now suppose that that individual came to hold a mistaken belief — say he believed there to be one less flower in the Santa Monica Canyon than in fact there is. Would we say that the individual in question had ceased to be the individual he was? That would seem counter-intuitive. Of course, this is not to suggest that the predicate 'omniscient' is not related to the title-term 'God' in such a way as to make 'God is omniscient' a necessary truth (Assumption I). What seems wrong is the *further* claim that the individual that bears the title 'God' (i.e., Yahweh) would not be the individual He is if He were not omniscient (Assumption IV). Let 'N(x) (If x is God then x is omniscient)' be true. What seems counter-intuitive is is that 'N(x)(If x is God then N (x is omniscient))' is also true.

(c) Boethius solves (or dissolves) the problem of divine foreknowledge by denying that God is a temporal being (Assumption V), and thus by denying that God holds beliefs about the outcome of human actions in advance of their performance (Assumption VI). On this account, God does not have genuine *fore*knowledge of human actions. This solution works (if it works at all) even if one holds that God

Timelessness, Foreknowledge and Free Will

is essentially omniscient and thus infallible in the strong sense used above. On the other hand, Augustine holds a view about the parallel between God's foreknowledge of human actions and ordinary human foreknowledge of those actions, that seems to require that we deny that God is infallible (in our strong sense) and thus that we deny that God is essentially omniscient (Assumption IV). This solution to the problem of divine foreknowledge is compatible with the idea that God is a temporal being (Assumption V) holding beliefs about the outcome of human actions in advance of their performance (Assumption VI). On this view, God could have genuine foreknowledge of natural events and human actions.[29]

The solutions offered by Boethius and Augustine to the problem of divine foreknowledge are interestingly different and yet interestingly similar. They are different in that they each involve an attack on a different item in the cluster of assumptions generating the problem. They are similar in that each involves an attack on one of the two equally basic assumptions that must be employed if the problem is to be formulated in a convincing way. As I mentioned at the outset, the problem of divine foreknowledge rests on two premises, *viz.*, that God is infallible and that God knows the outcome of human actions in advance of their performance. Given these two ideas (suitably interpreted), I am inclined to think that the problem is unavoidable. Boethius and Augustine – unlike Leibniz, Cicero and Prior – seem to me to have sensed the centre of the problem. I think that between the two of them they have exhausted the plausible channels out of this traditional perplexity.

NOTES

[1] An earlier version of this essay was published in the *Philosophical Review*, January 1965. I am indebted to John Turk Saunders of San Fernando State College and to Mrs. Marilyn McCord Adams for helping me to clarify my thinking on this topic. See Saunders's reply to my original article ('Of God and Freedom', *Philosophical Review*, January 1966), my rejoinder to Saunders ('Of God and Freedom: A Rejoinder', *Philosophical Review*, July

1966), and Mrs. Adams's comments on the argument between myself and Saunders ('Is the Existence of God a "Hard" Fact?', *Philosophical Review*, October 1967). I have also benefited greatly from a number of discussions with both Saunders and Adams.

[2] *Institutes of the Christian Religion*, Bk. III, Ch. XXI; this passage translated by John Allen (Philadelphia, 1813), II, 145.

[3] See ll. 140–75. Steward and Rand translation, pp. 409–11.

[4] *Consolation*, Bk. V, sec. 3, ll. 10–14.

[5] The notion of someone being *able* to do something and the notion of something being *within one's power* are essentially the same. Traditional formulations of the problem of divine foreknowledge (e.g., those of Boethius and Augustine) made use of the notion of what is (and what is not) *within one's power*. But the problem is the same when framed in terms of what one is (and one is not) *able* to do. Thus, I shall treat the statements 'Jones was able to do *x*', 'Jones had the ability to do *x*', and 'It was within Jones's power to do *x*' as equivalent. Richard Taylor, in 'I Can', *Philosophical Review*, LXIX (1960), 78–89, has argued that the notion of ability or power involved in these last three statements is incapable of philosophical analysis. Be that as it may, I shall not here attempt such an analysis. In what follows I shall, however, be careful to affirm only those statements about what is (or is not) within one's power that would have to be preserved on any analysis of this notion having even the most distant claim to adequacy.

[6] In Bk. II, Ch. XXI, secs. 8–11 of the *Essay*, John Locke says that an agent is not *free* with respect to a given action (i.e., that an action is done 'under necessity') when it is not within the agent's power to do otherwise. Locke allows a special kind of case, however, in which an action may be *voluntary* though done under necessity. If a man chooses to do something without knowing that it is not within his power to do otherwise (e.g., if a man chooses to stay in a room without knowing that the room is locked), his action may be voluntary though he is not free to forebear it. If Locke is right about this (and I shall not argue the point one way or the other) replace 'voluntary' with (let us say) 'free' in the discussion above and throughout the remainder of this chapter.

[7] *Theodicee*, Pt. I, sec. 37. This passage translated by E. M. Huggard (New Haven, 1952), p. 144. See also William Rowe's formulation and critique of the foreknowledge problem as discussed by St. Augustine in 'Foreknowledge and Free Will', *Review of Metaphysics*, 1964. Rowe's critique of the problem is very similar to the one offered by Leibniz in this passage.

[8] *De Libero Arbitrio*, Bk. III, Ch. 3, sec. 6. This passage translated by J. H. S. Burleigh, *Augustine's Earlier Writings* (Philadelphia, 1955).

[9] This passage translated by Marcus Dods, New York, Random House (Modern Library Series), 1950, pp. 153–4.

[10] *Summa Theologica*, Pt. I, Q. 14, A. 8.

[11] 'Formalities of Omniscience', *Philosophy*, 1962. The line of argument

just sketched is a summary of the central thrust of Prior's paper. Prior summarizes his position on pages 117–18. Some elements of this argument are expanded in Ch. VII of Prior's *Past, Present and Future* (Oxford, Clarendon Press, 1967). See especially sec. I.

[12] *Philosophical Review*, LXXI (1962), pp. 56–66. Taylor argues that if an event E fails to occur at T2, then at T1 it was true that E would fail to occur at T2. Thus, at T1, a necessary condition of anyone's performing an action sufficient for the occurrence of E at T2 is missing. Thus at T1, no one could have the power to perform an action that would be sufficient for the occurrence of E at T2. Hence, no one has the power at T1 to do something sufficient for the occurrence of an event at T2 that is not going to happen. The parallel between this argument and the one just recited can be seen very clearly if one reformulates Taylor's argument, pushing back the time at which it was true that E would not occur at T2.

[13] Richard Taylor develops this point in an article entitled 'Deliberation and Foreknowledge', *American Philosophical Quarterly*, January 1964. See especially p. 80.

[14] 'It Was To Be', *Dilemmas*, Cambridge, 1954.

[15] 'Endorsing Predications', *Philosophical Review*, 1961, pp. 367–78.

[16] 'Formalities of Omniscience', p. 124.

[17] *Ibid.*, pp. 121–2.

[18] For a helpful discussion of the difficulties involved in dating truth values, see Rogers Albritton's 'Present Truth and Future Contingency', a reply to Richard Taylor's 'The Problem of Future Contingency', both in the *Philosophical Review*, 1957.

[19] Bk. XI, Ch. 21. This passage translated by Marcus Dods (New York, Random House, 1950), p. 364.

[20] *Consolation*, Bk. V, sec. 6, ll. 75–80. This passage translated by Stewart and Rand, p. 405. See also Bk. V, sec. 6, ll. 60–70 and ll. 140–8.

[21] I interpret the phrase 'eternal-present' in accordance with the suggestion made at the end of the first chapter of this essay.

[22] *Consolation*, Bk. V, sec. 6, ll. 65–75. This passage translated by Stewart and Rand, pp. 404–5.

[23] This passage translated by J. H. S. Burleigh, *Augustine's Earlier Writings*, Philadelphia, 1955.

[24] Pt. I, sec. II, para. 55. This passage translated by W. R. Matthews, Edinburgh, 1928, p. 228.

[25] See the whole of Chs. 9 and 10.

[26] This passage translated by John Mourant, *Readings in the Philosophy of Religion*, New York, 1954, p. 426.

[27] *The Christian Doctrine of God*, translated by Olive Wyon, Philadelphia, 1964, p. 262.

[28] I argued in the second section of this chapter (subsections B and C) that the intermediate theses operating in the problem of divine foreknowledge as

formulated by Cicero and Prior are not operative in the problem of foreknowledge formulated in the first section of this chapter. I then concluded that the solutions to the problem offered by Cicero and Prior (which consisted in denying these intermediate theses) do nothing to alleviate the problem with which we are working. I should here like to offer another criticism of these two treatments of the topic. We saw above that Cicero and Prior solve the problem by denying what each takes to be the presupposition of foreknowledge as such. Their respective solutions preclude *human* foreknowledge as well as the foreknowledge of an omniscient being. I take this as the *reductio ad absurdum* of the positions they hold on this issue. Even if the foreknowledge did involve one or the other of the intermediate theses they deny (which it does not), neither of their solutions would be acceptable. Surely any adequate analysis of 'knowledge' and 'voluntary action' must allow that at least in some cases one can have knowledge of how another will voluntarily act in the future. This is precisely the point that Augustine, Schleiermacher, De Molina and Brunner are counting on in the passage cited above.

[29] I must acknowledge a difficulty with respect to each of the last two comments made about Augustine: (1) As regards the idea that God has genuine *fore*knowledge of human actions, in the *City of God* Augustine says emphatically that God knows all things *before* they come to pass (Bk. V, Ch. 9, italics mine). With respect to Cicero's contention that God does not have foreknowledge of human actions, Augustine describes this view as 'sacrilege', a product of the 'impious darings of reason'. Augustine says that he 'detests' this opinion – he adds:

> For either he (Cicero) denies that God exists . . . or if he confesses that He exists, but denies that He is prescient of future things what is that but just 'the fool saying in his heart there is no God?' For one who is not prescient of all future things is not God (Bk. V, Ch. 9. Dods's translation, pp. 154–6).

I think it must be admitted that this position is incompatible with what is said in the long passage cited from the *City of God* on p. 73. In that passage Augustine was surely saying that neither God nor His cognitions can be assigned position in time relative to the things He knows. Augustine's remarks on the topic of foreknowledge seem clearly to entail that God's cognitions have temporal position, i.e., that they are located *prior* to the things He knows. (2) With respect to my suggestion that Augustine's insistence on the parallel between human foreknowledge and God's foreknowledge commits him to the idea that omniscience is not one of God's *essential* properties, I think it must also be admitted that this commitment conflicts with Augustine's claim that *all* of God's properties are essential. As we saw in the first section of Ch. II, for Augustine, the Supreme Being 'has not anything' it can lose. I don't know what to say about these discrepancies. It may be that what Augustine says when dealing with the problem of divine foreknowledge is just plainly inconsistent with what he says in other parts of his theological texts.

5
Timeless Knowledge of What is Happening Now

A number of contemporary philosophers have said that there is logical conflict between the idea that God is timeless and the idea that God is omniscient. If a given individual is timeless (so it is urged), that individual could not be omniscient because there is a limited, though important, range of facts that a timeless being could not know. Of course, an omniscient being is one that knows *all* facts. It follows that if an individual is timeless, that individual is not omniscient. In this chapter I want to examine the argument given for this position.

What kinds of things could a timeless being know?

Could a timeless being know that, e.g., two plus two equals four? In the case where the item known is a fact such as two plus two equals four, it might be sensible to describe an individual as having knowledge while denying that the individual in question has temporal extension or temporal position. Let us assume that this is sensible (I shall examine this assumption in sec. II of Ch. 7). The philosophers I want to discuss in this chapter have not challenged this possibility. So far as their remarks are concerned, there is no logical difficulty in the idea of a timeless knower as such.

Knowing that two plus two equals four is knowing a fact (of sorts), but the fact in question is not what one would call a 'temporal fact'. The description of the item known requires no mention of temporal relations or temporal extension. Now consider the fact that, e.g., Abraham Lincoln was assassinated sometime after the Battle of Gettysburg. This is a 'temporal fact' in the sense just explained. Could a timeless being know facts of this sort? Again, the philosophers I want to discuss in this chapter have not challenged this possibility. Boethius said that God 'beholds' the whole matrix of temporally ordered events and circumstances. God does not behold them one after another; He grasps them in a single act of cognition. God knows every detail of the temporally ordered matrix – including all of the temporal relations between the events and circumstances involved. But, of course, God's cognition is not, itself, temporally qualified. Though God is aware *of* temporal events, His awareness is not, itself, a temporal event. (Recall the distinction made in the first chapter of this essay between the awareness of time and the time of awareness.) For present purposes, we can assume that this line of thinking is acceptable.

Could a timeless being know that today is the seventeenth of July? Here is where the issue begins. In a later portion of the article discussed at length in the last chapter,[1] Arthur Prior claims that a fact such as the fact that today is the seventeenth of July could not be known by a timeless being. Since this fact is a fact, it would have to be known by any being who knows all facts – i.e., an omniscient being. It follows that if a given individual is timeless, that individual cannot be omniscient. The following passage is taken from an article entitled 'Professor Malcolm on God' by Robert Coburn. It is the clearest formulation I have found of the argument first offered by Prior. Using 'eternal' to mean 'timeless', Coburn writes as follows:[2]

> If a being is omniscient, then presumably it follows that this being knows everything which (logically) can be known. But it is easy to see that an eternal being could not know everything which (logically) can be known, and this is because some of the facts which (logically) can be known, are knowable only by temporal beings, by beings who occupy some position (or some positions) in time.

Timeless Knowledge of What is Happening Now

> Consider, for example, the fact that the day which is now elapsing (I write this on May 12, 1962) is May 12, 1962; or more simply, that today is May 12, 1962. Clearly to know this fact is tantamount to knowing one's temporal position, and being oriented in time. But if this is true, then a necessary condition of knowing this fact, it would seem, is having some position in time concerning which there are truths of the type indicated to be known. To see the matter in another light, assume that the idea of a non-temporal knower makes sense. Then ask, could such a knower know, e.g., that today in May 12, 1962? The obvious answer, I submit, is that it could only if it could use temporal indicator words. For otherwise, it could not express and *a fortiori* could not entertain a truth such as the above. But a necessary condition of being able to use temporal indicator words is being an occupant of time. Hence, God's alleged eternity is logically incompatible with his alleged omniscience.

Coburn says that to know the fact that today is the twelfth of May is 'tantamount to knowing one's temporal position'. It follows, he points out, that a necessary condition of knowing that today is the twelfth of May is that one have a temporal position – more specifically, that one exist on the twelfth of May. So far this argument seems to me to be correct. However, Coburn now concludes that there is a 'truth' that a timeless being could not entertain or know. The 'truth' in question is that today is the twelfth of May. The reason why a timeless being could not know this 'truth' is that he does not have location in time, i.e., he does not exist on the twelfth of May. I think that this conclusion has not been adequately argued.

Consider the following game: There are ten men in a room. On the floor of the room are painted two large circles. Five men stand in each circle. One at a time, the names of the men in the room are flashed on a screen. The men take turns locating the man whose name appears on the screen. If Jones is in the circle occupied by Smith and if it is Smith's turn to play, then if Jones's name appears on the screen the correct response for Smith to make would be, 'Jones is here'. If Jones is in the other circle, the correct response for Smith to make would be, 'Jones is there'. Responses of the form, 'ϕ is here' and 'ϕ is there' are the only ones open to the players. Now, let's introduce an observer watching the game from outside of the room. Call him Brown. Brown could not participate in the game. If *his* name were to be flashed on the screen, neither 'Brown is here' nor 'Brown is there' would be a correct response for Smith to make. And if Jones's name were flashed on the screen, neither 'Jones is here' nor 'Jones is there' would be a correct response for Brown to make. Still, Brown could keep the score of the game. Though his spatial position places him outside of the game-discourse, he could understand the discourse and could know the facts that determine whether or not a correct response had been made by a given player in a given turn.

Now let's suppose that Smith and Jones are in the same circle, that Jones's name appears on the screen, and it is Smith's turn to respond. Smith says: 'Jones is here.' The outside observer (Brown) says: 'Jones and Smith are in the same circle.' We ask both Smith and Brown to *justify* their respective assertions. Both call attention to the same circumstance, *viz*., the relative spatial position of Jones and Smith. Unless given an argument to the contrary, it would seem reasonable to suppose that both had reported the same fact. Shall we then say that the sentence, 'Jones is here', and the sentence, 'Jones and Smith are in the same circle', have the same meaning? But 'Jones is here' makes no mention of Smith nor does it contain reference to the circle. Perhaps we should say that in this situation, a complete meaning analysis of 'Jones is here' would include mention of the fact that it was uttered by Smith in the context of the game. When this is made explicit (the argument continues) it will be seen that 'Jones is here' and 'Jones and Smith are in the same circle' have the same meaning in this case. I'm not sure what to say about this last suggestion. I do not have an analysis to propose for statements containing indexical expressions such as 'here'. But whatever the truth may be as regards the issue about meaning, I'm still inclined to think that Smith and Brown have reported the same fact in their different ways. If we should say that their utterances do not have the same meaning, the conclusion would have to be that in some situations (especially those involving use of indexical language) statements having different meanings can be used to report the same fact.

Before commenting directly on Coburn's remarks about the statement 'Today is the twelfth of May', I should like to consider the argument presented in the following passage from Norman Kretzmann's article 'Omniscience and Immutability'. (I shall not try to comment on the major thesis of Kretzmann's paper since this would take us too far afield.)[3]

> According to (one) familiar account of omniscience, the knowledge an omniscient being has of the entire scheme of contingent events is in many relevant respects exactly like the knowledge you might have of a movie you had written, directed, produced, starred in and seen a thousand times. You would know its every scene in flawless detail, and you would have the length of each scene and the sequence of scenes perfectly in mind. You would know, too, that a clock pictured in the first scene shows the time to be 3.45 and that a clock pictured in the fourth scene shows 4.30, and so on. Suppose, however, that your movie is being shown in a distant theatre today. You know the movie immeasurably better than do the people in the theatre who are now seeing it for the first time, but they know one big thing about it you don't know, namely, what is now going on on the screen. Thus, the similar account of omniscience regarding contingent events is drastically incomplete. An omniscient being must know not only the entire scheme of contingent events from beginning to end at once, but also *at which stage of realization that scheme is now.*

What would it be for me (as author, producer, etc., of the play) to know that the first scene is *now* appearing on the screen? What would have to be true in order for me to say correctly: 'The first scene is now on the screen'? For this statement to be true, I would have to be uttering these words at the time when the first scene is on the screen. If I were to utter them at some other time (e.g., when the second scene was on the screen), my utterance would be false – it could not be counted as reporting a fact or as formulating an item of knowledge. Now, let's suppose that a timeless individual says: 'The first scene is now on the screen.' Coburn says that a timeless being could not make use of sentences utilizing temporal indexical expressions such as 'today' or 'now'. But I can find no reason to think this is true. A timeless being might say: 'The first scene is *now* on the screen.' The only consequence would be that the proposition he would be asserting would be false. When uttered by a given individual, this sentence entails something about the temporal position of the speaker relative to the occurrence of the first scene on the screen. If uttered by an individual lacking temporal position, it would thus, of necessity, be false.

Shall we then conclude that there is a fact (*viz.*, the fact that the first scene is on the screen) that a timeless individual could not know or report? A timeless individual might know that at a certain point in time, the first scene was on the screen. He might identify this temporal point in a variety of ways. He might say, for example, that it was 3.47 p.m. on the sixth of September. In order to pin it down in a different way, he might add that it was the moment at which Pike said: 'The first scene is now on the screen.' Let's suppose that the timeless individual makes use of both of these identifications. He says: 'At 3.47 p.m. on the sixth of September – the moment at which Pike said "the first scene is now on the screen" – the first scene was on the screen.' Would the timeless individual have reported the same fact as I reported when I said: 'The first scene is now on the screen'? Let's agree that the sentence uttered by the timeless individual would not have the same meaning as the one I used in my report. I'm not really sure that this is true – since the correct analysis of 'the first scene is now on the screen' might have to make mention of the fact that it was uttered by Pike at a certain time (however that time is to be identified) – but let's grant this assumption for the sake of argument. Still, I can find no reason for thinking that I and the timeless individual have not reported the same fact. If called upon later to justify my original comment, I would point to the fact that at 3.47 p.m. on the sixth of September — the moment at which I said: 'The first scene is now on the screen' — the first scene was on the screen. This is precisely what the timeless being would point to if challenged to justify his report. Even if we grant that the utterances under consideration do not have the same meaning (which is an assumption I shall not try to evaluate), we would not have enough to conclude that they are not reports of the same fact. As mentioned above, it might be that in some situations (especially those involving use of indexical language) sentences having different meanings can be used to report the same facts.

If, on the twelfth of May, one says: 'Today is the twelfth of May', what one says is true. But if, on the seventeenth of July, one says: 'Today is the twelfth of May', what one says is false. Now, let's ask whether there is a fact reported in the passage cited earlier from Coburn that *I* could not know and report. I could know and report that as Coburn was writing the passage cited above (the one in which he said: 'Today is the twelfth of May') it was, in fact, the twelfth of May. But, if *I* were to report this fact, I could not use the form of words used by Coburn. I could not say: 'Today is the twelfth of May'. If I were to say this, I would not be reporting a fact at all. Today is the seventeenth of July. However, I could report that a certain day was, in fact, the twelfth of May. I might identify the day in question in a variety of ways. I might say that it was the day so and so many days after the turn of the year, or so and so many days after the birth of Christ. I might also specify it as the day upon which Coburn wrote: 'Today is the twelfth of May.' Let us suppose that I report as follows: 'The day so and so many days after the turn of the year (or so and so many days after the birth of Christ) — the day upon which Coburn wrote: "Today is the twelfth of May" — was the twelfth of May.' As above, we might want to admit that this sentence does not have the same meaning as the one used by Coburn in his report. But, as above, it is not at all clear that this sentence could not be used to report the same fact as was

God and Timelessness

reported by Coburn when he said: 'Today is the twelfth of May.' If asked to justify our respective assertions, both of us would call attention to the same circumstance, *viz.*, that the day so and so many days after the turn of the year (or after the birth of Christ) – the day upon which Coburn said: 'Today is the twelfth of May' – was, in fact, the twelfth of May.

Let's imagine that a timeless individual says: 'Today is the twelfth of May.' What he said would be false. If one says: 'Today is the twelfth of May', what one says can be true only if one occupies a certain temporal position at the time of the utterance. Since a timeless individual has no temporal position, he could not make use of this form of words when articulating a true proposition. Coburn's conclusion is that there is a 'truth' that a timeless individual could not know or report. The 'truth' in question is the one Coburn formulated in the sentence, 'Today is the twelfth of May'. Coburn rightly sees that when he (Coburn) wrote: 'Today is the twelfth of May', what he said was true. He also sees that the truth therein reported would have to be known by any individual who knows everything. However, Coburn would probably allow that a timeless individual could have an item of knowledge that he (the timeless individual) could report in the sentence: 'The day so and so many days after the turn of the year (or so and so many days after the birth of Christ) – the day upon which Coburn wrote: "Today is the twelfth of May" – was the twelfth of May.' For the reasons given above in connection with the other cases just treated, even if we were to admit that the sentence written by Coburn and the sentence uttered by the timeless being do not have the same meaning, I don't think we could conclude that Coburn and the timeless being had not reported the same fact.

I'll summarize the line of argument I have tried to develop in this chapter as follows:

A timeless individual could not have an item of knowledge that *he* could formulate or report in a statement such as, 'The first scene is now on the screen' or 'Today is the twelfth of

Timeless Knowledge of What is Happening Now

May'. This is because statements of this sort serve (in part) to identify the temporal position of the speaker relative to some event or circumstance such as, e.g., the occurrence of the first scene on the screen, the first of the year, the birth of Christ, etc. (Model this point in the ten man game. In the game, 'Jones is here', served to identify the spatial position of the speaker relative to the spatial position of Jones.) I cannot see, however, that this observation gives warrant for the claim that there is something that a timeless individual could not know. As uttered by a timeless being, statements such as, 'The first scene is now on the screen' and 'Today is the twelfth of May' do not report facts at all. There is nothing here that *could be known* – either by the timeless being *or by anyone else*. Of course, as uttered by a *temporal* being, statements of this sort sometimes report facts. But we have not been given a reason for thinking that the facts in question could not be reported by a timeless being in statements free of temporal indexical expressions. Two things have not been shown: (1) that true statements in which temporal indexical expressions are used (e.g., 'Today is the twelfth of May', as uttered by Coburn on the twelfth of May) cannot be formulated in statements having equivalent meanings but which are free of temporal indexical expressions; and (2) that if there are no such meaning-equivalent formulations of statements utilizing temporal indexical expressions, the facts reported in these statements cannot be reported in statements free of indexical expressions. Thus, so far as has been effectively argued to the contrary, what is known by a timeless being might well exhaust the class of knowable facts. (Keep in mind that in the ten man game, the outside observer could keep the score of the game.) Prior, Coburn and Kretzmann claim to have identified a range of facts that a timeless individual could not know. But this claim has not been established. So far as I can determine, all that has been established is that there are certain *forms of words* that a timeless individual could not use when formulating or reporting his knowledge.

God and Timelessness

NOTES

[1] 'The Formalities of Omniscience', *Philosophy*, 1962, p. 116.

[2] 'Professor Malcolm on God', *Australasian Journal of Philosophy*, August 1963, pp. 155–6.

[3] 'Omniscience and Immutability', *Journal of Philosophy*, July 1966, p. 414.

6
Timelessness and Power

In this chapter I shall examine some of the logical relations between the doctrine of God's timelessness and each of three standard Christian doctrines that centre on the idea of God's power, *viz*., (1) the doctrine of omnipotence, (2) the doctrine of divine creation, and (3) the doctrine of divine preservation.

I

Schleiermacher says that eternity (timelessness) is an 'inactive attribute'. To think of God as eternal is to think of Him as idle and inert. He adds that this is not an adequate picture of the Christian God. The trouble here, Schleiermacher says, is that the doctrine of eternity cannot be considered apart from the doctrine of omnipotence. Omnipotence is an 'active attribute'. To think of God as omnipotent is to think of Him as vital and effective. Of course, Schleiermacher continues, the doctrine of omnipotence would also be inadequate if considered by itself. It needs to be accompanied by the doctrine of eternity. Eternity and omnipotence are antithetical, though mutually supplementary attributes. Each corrects the distortion that the other would have if considered by itself.[1] Schleiermacher writes:[2]

> Instead, therefore, of saying that God is eternal and almighty, we should say, rather, that He is almighty-eternal and eternal-almighty, or that God is eternal omnipotence or almighty eternity.

Let's look at what Schleiermacher has to say about God's omnipotence.

Pre-analytically, to say that a given individual is omnipotent is to say that that individual has unlimited power. This is usually expressed in religious discourse with the phrase 'infinite power'. St. Thomas explicated the intuitive content of this idea in the formula: 'God is called omnipotent because He can do all things that are possible absolutely.'[3] Shall we then say that God can swim the English Channel? As we have seen (Ch. 3), if God is timeless, He is also incorporeal. Nothing an incorporeal being could do would count as swimming the English Channel. This last point can be generalized. Nothing an incorporeal being could do would count as jumping a fence, riding a bike, etc. (All of this was made clear by Peter Lombard in *The Sentences*: I, d. 42, Ch. 2.) However, St. Thomas need not be interpreted as claiming that God can do all things possible absolutely in the sense that He can perform any kind of action (such as, e.g., swimming, jumping or bike-riding). Thomas's formula is usually given a relatively restricted interpretation. The permissive verb 'do' in 'do all things possible absolutely' is usually replaced with one of a class of more limited verbs – a class that includes 'create', 'bring about', 'affect', 'produce', 'make-to-be', and the like.[4] God's omnipotence is thus to be thought of as creative power only. It is not to be understood as the ability to perform all kinds of actions. God is omnipotent in that He can create, bring about, affect, produce, make-to-be, etc., anything possible absolutely. For St. Thomas, something is 'possible absolutely' when its description is logically consistent. Thus, on the finished analysis, God is omnipotent in that He can bring about any consistently desirable state of affairs. In his article on 'Omnipotent' in the *Catholic Encyclopedia*,[5] J. A. McHugh analysed the notion in this way. It is reasonably clear from the context of this piece that McHugh meant to be reformulating St. Thomas's view of the matter. I might add that I think this restricted interpretation of the pre-analytical notion of infinite power is an accurate portrayal of the way this concept works in the ordinary, as well as in most of the technical (theological) discourse of the Christian religion.

Schleiermacher acknowledges that as traditionally under stood, the notion of omnipotence is the notion of '... the ability to effect all that is possible or all which contains no contradiction in itself'.[6] However, Schleiermacher insists that this analysis is inadequate. The trouble here, he says, is that this analysis presupposes a distinction between what God is *able* to do and what God *does*. When dealing with an ordinary individual, such a distinction is legitimate and important. But this distinction has no application when dealing with God. Schleiermacher provides two arguments for this last claim.[7] First, in the usual case, the class of things one does is limited relative to the class of things one can do. Schleiermacher says that no such limitation can be assigned to God. Secondly, Schleiermacher suggests that the gap between one's having the ability to do something and one's actually doing the thing in question is one that is filled by what he calls an 'individual impulse' having its cause 'from without'. With respect to God, there is no such thing as an 'individual impulse'; and it would be wrong to suppose that God could ever be caused to act by something 'from without'. Though both of these arguments seem to me to be utterly obscure, the conclusion Schleiermacher thinks they support is clearly stated in the text. God has no ability that he does not exercise. Thus, instead of analysing the notion of infinite power in terms of God's ability, we should analyse this concept in terms of God's activity.

What, then, of God's activity? Picture the universe as a single matrix of events, circumstances, situations, etc. Each item in the matrix has a cause within the matrix itself. God is active with respect to the matrix as a whole. And what activity is involved here? Schleiermacher says that God *sustains* or *preserves* the entire matrix considered as a unit. The universe as a whole is 'absolutely dependent' on God. On Schleiermacher's view, to say that God is omnipotent is to say that He is the omni-preserver. God is the sustaining cause of the universe considered as a whole.

God and Timelessness

I think it is worth noting that a line of thinking in some respects similar to this one is developed by St. Anselm in his comments on the notion of eternity. As we have seen (Ch. 1), Anselm says that God is not to be located in time or space. Yet, just a few pages prior to the passage in which he denies the appropriateness of temporal and special predicates when applied to God, Anselm says that God must exist 'in every time and place'.[8] He says that since everything depends on God for its existence, where God does not exist, nothing exists. Anselm concludes:[9]

> In no place or time, then, is this being properly said to exist, since it is contained by no other at all. And yet it may be said after a manner of its own, to be in every place and time, since whatever else exists is sustained by its presence lest it laps into nothingness.

Although temporal and special predicates do not apply to God, He may be said *'after a manner of His own'*, to exist in every time and place. And what manner is this? The point may be that God exists in every place and at every time in the sense that His sustaining power is evident in every time and place. God exists in Los Angeles at four o'clock not in the sense that He is within the city limits at that time, but in the sense that Los Angeles would not exist at four o'clock were it not for God's sustaining activity. (This interpretation of Anselm's remarks seems to be confirmed in the two paragraphs immediately preceding the passage cited above.) Ask this question: Does God have temporal location? The answer is no and yes (in a sense). God is not temporally qualified, but nothing that is temporally qualified would exist were it not for God's sustaining power. Of course, there is no reason to think that Anselm would accept Schleiermacher's 'reduction' of the concept of omnipotence to the concept of God's sustaining activity. But it might be that Anselm would accept Schleiermacher's idea that the notion of eternity and the notion of God's sustaining activity are closely related (even mutually supplementary) concepts.

Timelessness and Power

II

Schleiermacher rejected the traditional analysis of the predicate 'omnipotent' on the grounds that no distinction can be made between the idea of God's ability and the idea of God's activity. However, there is a second theme running through Schleiermacher's reflections on the topic of omnipotence that seems to me to provide a more helpful explanation of his reluctance to accept the traditional analysis of this concept. This second theme rests on the idea that a being that is omnipotent in the traditional sense of 'omnipotent' must have a position in time. I want now to work on this thesis—Schleiermacher makes only sketchy suggestions concerning its rationale. I'll begin with three preliminary remarks about Schleiermacher's reflections on the doctrine of divine creation.

(1) According to traditional Christian thinking, God created the world of natural objects. Focus for a moment on the verb that occurs in the standard formulation of this doctrine. There are a number of features of the idea expressed by this verb that set it aside from other ideas that are usually expressed by verbs marking deliberate or intentional productive activity.

First, God created the world out of nothing. This is to say that God used no pre-existing materials in its production. Thus 'created' in 'God created the world' lacks one of the normal implications of a production-verb such as 'built'. If one builds a bird-house, one uses materials such as tin or wood. One could not build something unless one had something out of which to build it. God could not have *built* the universe out of nothing. In this regard 'created' in 'God created the world' seems to work like the verb 'conjured' in 'Jones conjured up a mental image of his mother'. It might also be compared with 'uttered' in 'Jones uttered the word "dog" '. If one conjures up a mental image or utters a word, one produces something; but one does not produce the thing in question out of pre-existing materials. There is nothing out of which one makes a mental image or an articulate sound. If one had a taste for dramatic expression, one might say that mental images and articulate sounds are 'created out of nothing'.

Second, God created the world without benefit of tools or instruments. No devices were used in its production. In this respect, 'created' in 'God created the world' differs from a production-verb such as 'chiselled' in 'Jones chiselled his name in the stone'. Unless one had a tool (a chisel or something like a chisel) one could not chisel his name in the stone. Again in this regard, 'created' in 'God created the world' shares a feature with 'conjured' and 'uttered'. When one conjures up a mental image or when one utters a sound, one does not do so by manipulating tools or instruments. Of course, when one utters a sound, one uses one's mouth and lips. But I doubt if one's mouth and lips should be counted as tools used in the production of a sound. When one dances, one uses one's arms and legs. But ones' arms and legs are not tools by which one dances a dance.

Third, since God is incorporeal, the act whereby He brought the world into existence must have been performed without bodily organs or appendages. At this point, we should distinguish 'created' in 'God created the world' from 'uttered' in 'Jones uttered the word "dog" '. In order to utter a word, one must have a mouth (or something like a mouth). However, 'conjured' in 'Jones conjured up a mental image' still provides a parallel on this point. Though I doubt that one could conjure up a mental image unless one had a brain, it is not at all clear that this reveals a *logical* feature of 'conjured'. A disembodied mind might conjure up a mental image.

Up to this point, it would appear that 'conjured' in 'Jones conjured up a mental image' is closer to 'created' in 'God created the world' than are any of the other production-verbs so far mentioned. But there may be a difference between 'conjured' and 'created' that would be of some importance if it could be established. It might be that the product of the conjuring activity (i.e., the mental image), is not to be distinguished from the conjuring activity itself. On this view, the product of the conjuring activity is less the *product* of the activity than it is the activity itself described in 'thing' rather than 'action' language. One adds 'a mental image' to 'conjured' only in order to identify the *kind* of conjuring involved — not in order to identify the product of the conjuring action. If we could accept this account (and I'm not really sure that we should), we would have to distinguish the notion expressed by 'conjured' in 'Jones conjured up a mental image' from the notion expressed by 'created' in 'God created the world'. The traditional Christian position is that the world is a genuine product of the divine creative act. It is not the divine creative-act itself described in 'thing' rather than 'action' language. Given these reflections, 'created' in 'God created the world' begins to look like 'built' in 'Jones built a birdhouse'. What one builds is clearly distinguishable from one's building-action. Perhaps the closest parallel we have in our little collection of production-verbs is 'uttered'. The sound produced when one utters a word is distinguishable from the action named by 'uttered'. In this regard, 'uttered' is like 'built' and unlike 'conjured'. But, 'uttered' is like 'conjured' and unlike 'built' in that it does not entail (or suggest) the use of pre-existing materials. 'Uttered' is also like 'conjured' and unlike, e.g., 'chiselled', in that it does not suggest the use of tools or instruments. 'Uttered' fails, where 'conjured' does not, in that it applies only in cases involving use of a bodily organ.

According to Martin Luther, the creation-relation that obtains between God and the world is to be modelled on the creation-relation that obtains between a speaker (or a speaking-action) and the words or articulated sounds that he utters. Luther said: 'What is the whole creation else than a word of God, said and spoken by God? . . . thus it is for God no harder to create than for us to speak.' Schleiermacher quotes this passage with approval. He adds: '. . . the world itself, since it came into existence through the spoken word, is the word of God.'[10] It seems to me that we are here receiving instructions about the logic of the verb 'created' in the statement 'God created the world'. We are being told that 'created' is to be understood as parallel with the production-verb 'uttered'. In a later passage Schleiermacher corrects for that part of the logic of 'uttered' that lacks parallel with 'created', i.e., he corrects for the fact that one can utter a word only if one possesses a bodily organ. He writes:[11]

> And since in God there is no duality between thought and word (nay, even the term 'word' can only mean the activity of thought outwards), this precisely is the point expressed in all formulae which exhibit the divine Word as creating and preserving; and it is quite correct to say, as has been said in multifarious ways, that everything exists by reason of God's speaking it or thinking it.

(Note that in this passage the term 'word' is said to stand for the divine creative-activity itself and not for the *product* of that activity as was the case in the passage in which Schleiermacher, following Luther, described the world itself as the word of God.) I think that the point we are to gather from these passages taken together is that the divine creative-activity is to be understood as a kind of logical 'cross' between a speaking-action and a thinking-action. Schleiermacher wants those logical features of 'uttered' and 'thought' (or 'conjured') wherein they are different from 'built' and 'chiselled' as regards the use of pre-existing materials and tools. He wants that part of the logic of 'thought' (or 'conjured') whereby it is free of implications regarding the use of bodily organs (unlike 'uttered'); and he wants that part of the logic of 'uttered' whereby it may differ from 'thought' (or 'conjured') as regards the independence of the item produced and the creative-activity by which it is produced.

(2) Let us suppose that yesterday a mountain, 17,000 feet high, came into existence on the flatlands of Illinois. One of the local theists explains this occurrence by reference to divine creative action. He claims that God produced (created, brought about) the mountain. Of course, if God is timeless, He could not have produced the mountain *yesterday*. This would require that God's creative-activity and thus

Timelessness and Power

the individual whose activity it is have position in time. The theist's claim is that God *timelessly* brought it about that yesterday, a 17,000 feet high mountain came into existence on the flatlands of Illinois. Schleiermacher would reject this explanation of the mountain phenomenon. According to his account, every temporal circumstance or state of affairs has a complete cause *within* the temporal matrix.[12] On the question of whether God might produce something like the mountain we are imagining, Schleiermacher writes as follows:[13]

> ... the divine omnipotence can never in any way enter as a supplement (so to speak) to the natural causes in their sphere; for then it must like them work temporarily and spatially; and at one time working so, and then again, not so, it would not be self-identical and so would be neither eternal nor omnipotence.

The point seems to be that if God were to create or produce an object having position in time, God's creative activity would then have to have occurred at some specific time. The claim that God *timelessly* produced a temporal object (such as the mountain) is absurd. Given that God is timeless, Schleiermacher concludes, '... it is inadmissible to suppose that any time anything should begin to be through omnipotence'.[14]

If I know that Jones built a bird-house, I know that the building-action occurred prior to the existence of the finished bird-house. The bird-house counts as finished only *after* the last piece has been nailed into place. The same would hold if I knew that Jones chiselled his name in the stone, painted a picture, wrote a story, moulded a nickel out of lead, etc. In each of these cases, the production-verb carries clear implications regarding the temporal position of the product relative to the creative-activity involved in its production. (Cases of this sort may well have been among those that Hume considered when he arrived at the conclusion that causes must precede their effects in time.)

Suppose that at a certain time (T) a certain thought or mental image occurs. Let us also suppose that the thought or mental image was thought, or conjured up by Jones. If one were to ask about the temporal position of Jones's thinking-activity, we could answer the question without hesitation. The thinking-action occurred at T. The temporal position of the thought or mental image *is* the temporal position of the thinking-activity in question. In this case, the following argument is (informally) valid:

(1) Jones thought (or conjured up) x
(2) x occurred at T
(3) ∴ At T, Jones thought (or conjured up) x

It seems to me that a pattern of argument very much like this one will hold as well for the case of uttering a sound. If I am sitting across the table from Jones and I hear an articulate sound at T, then if Jones uttered the sound, he uttered the sound at T. This last sentence formulates the criterion we use when attempting to determine when Jones spoke. The speaking-action begins when the sound begins – it is not speaking-action until the sound begins. Barring echoes, radios, recording, etc., the speaking-action ends when the sound can no longer be heard by an auditor sitting across the table. (Cases of this sort might well have been among the ones Kant considered when arguing that in some instances, causes do not precede their effects in time – sometimes causes and effects are simultaneous.)[15]

The specialized verbs we use when describing a case of deliberate or intentional production (e.g., 'builds', 'chiselled', 'writes', 'painted', etc.) seem to carry with them identifiable implications regarding the relative temporal positions of the items produced and the creative-activity involved in their production. This seems to be true of production-verbs in general and, of particular interest to us, it is also true of the verbs 'utters' and 'thinks' (or 'conjures') – the two production-verbs having special significance when attempting to explicate the import of the verb occurring in sentences of the form 'God created (or produced) x'. It would appear that if we can assign a temporal location to what one produces, by the logic of 'produces', as revealed in the logic of the specialized verbs falling under this determinable, we can assign relative temporal position to the productive-activity itself.

Might we not cancel the temporal implications of 'produces' just as we eliminated other unwanted implications of this verb in the preceding discussion? We were able to direct attention away from the idea of pre-existing materials and tools by modelling 'produces' after 'conjures' and 'utters' rather than after 'builds' and 'chisels'. We were able to direct attention away from the idea of bodily organs and appendages by modelling 'produces' after 'conjures' rather than 'utters'; and when confronted with the fact (if it is a fact) that the product of the conjuring-activity cannot be distinguished from the activity itself; we switched the model back to 'utters'. Might we not do the same with respect to the *temporal* implications of 'produces'? The trouble with this suggestion is that the determinable verb 'produces', unlike the specialized verbs falling under it, does not have these *other* unwanted implications. We were able to pull attention away from these other implications by moving around *within* the class of production-verbs. The same does not seem to be true of the temporal implications. They seem to be there in every case; they seem to be part of the 'essence' of 'produces'. I think it was this realization that led Schleiermacher to the view that God could not create, produce or bring about a temporal state of affairs. I think that this was the reason behind his insistence that '. . . it is inadmissible to suppose that at any time something should begin to be through omnipotence'.

(3) But we have a problem. If something is produced, created or brought into being, it *begins* to exist. To produce something is to effect its beginning. Further, as we noted in sec. I of Ch. III (subsection *C*), if something begins to exist, it has position in time. Thus, if something is produced or created, it has position in time. If Schleiermacher holds that God cannot produce objects or states of affairs having position in time, he must then hold that God can produce nothing whatsoever. Everything produced or created must

have position in time. But, surely, no Christian theologian could deny that God created *something*. Leaving aside the case of the 17,000 feet high mountain in Illinois, how about the universe considered as a whole? What's going to happen to the traditional doctrine of divine creation?

According to Schleiermacher, the traditional doctrine of divine creation is shot through with elements that are foreign to religious interests. The Mosaic account of creation is an effort to explain the origin of finite being. It is a mythological speculation introduced in order to satiate our 'curiosity' or, at best, our thirst for historical knowledge. It provides a primitive answer to what is, properly, a 'scientific' question.[16] Schleiermacher seems to acknowledge that as formulated in the traditional account of creation, the claim that God created the world implies that the world had a beginning in time.[17] It thus implies (Schleiermacher seems to agree) that God's creative-activity has temporal location. He writes:[18]

> But in so far as the idea of creation in time must be related to that of a beginning of divine activity *ad extra* or a beginning of the divine sovereignty as Origen suggested, God would be brought into the region of change and subjected to time.

Schleiermacher says that the Mosaic myth concerning the origin of finite being can be safely deleted from serious theology. It is primitive science, and is not relevant to religion. Further, Schleiermacher seems to hold that this myth *must* be so deleted. As it stands it entails that God's creative activity had position in time. However, Schleiermacher maintains that under-pinning the traditional account of the notion of creation is a genuine religious insight that cannot be deleted from theology. It is the same insight that is more directly expressed in the doctrine of divine *preservation*. When properly understood, Schleiermacher says, the doctrine of divine creation and the doctrine of divine preservation are 'equivalent' – they are, in fact, one and the same doctrine.[19] What the doctrine of creation emphasizes is that the notion of preservation involved in the doctrine of preservation has a productive or creative aspect. When one sustains something (in the sense intended in this doctrine) one is not engaged in a passive action. The act of preservation is a kind of creative 'outpouring'. As he did with respect to the divine of omnipotence, Schleiermacher seems here to be 'reducing' the doctrine of divine creation to the doctrine of divine preservation. However, a trace of the notion of creation remains. The verbs 'preserves' and 'sustains' are to be understood as having productive overtones.

At this point, I should like to add just two brief comments about the position Schleiermacher takes on the traditional doctrine of divine creation.

First, since on Schleiermacher's account, the doctrine of creation and the doctrine of preservation are equivalent in content, it is likely that the instuctions we received (and reviewed above) for understanding the verb 'created' in 'God created the world' will be relevant when attempting to grasp Schleiermacher's understanding of the verb 'preserves' in 'God preserves the world'. When we come to the problem of interpreting the doctrine of preservation, the 'utteredthought' model developed above will probably have to play a role in our thinking.

Secondly, it is clear that in Schleiermacher's opinion, the notion of preservation does not carry the unfortunate temporal implications that we found to be connected with the notion of creation. So far as I can see, it was largely the temporal implications of 'creates' that led Schleiermacher to 'reduce' the idea expressed by this verb to the idea expressed by 'preserves'. The assumption must be (as indeed it is)[20] that when propositions of the form 'x preserves y' are properly understood, they will be seen to differ from propositions of the form 'x created y' in that the former, unlike the latter, carry no implications regarding temporal relations between x and y. We can get a glimpse of this already. As Schleiermacher points out, 'x preserves y', unlike 'x creates y' does not entail that y had a beginning.[21] It thus does not, itself, entail that x's activity with respect to *y* had a beginning. I shall expand and examine this thesis in the next section of this chapter.

I think we can now identify what may have been the real (though subterranean) reason why Schleiermacher rejected the traditional interpretation of the notion of divine omnipotence. A timeless individual could not *produce*, *create*, or *bring about* an object, circumstance, or state of affairs. If the reasoning set forth above is correct, this would be true whether dealing with a specific finite object such as the mountain in Illinois or with the total complex of finite objects constituting the universe considered as a unit. It would also be true even if we restricted attention to objects, circumstances and states of affairs having logically consistent descriptions (there are no others). It follows that a timeless individual could not be omnipotent given the traditional interpretation of the predicate 'omnipotent'. If it makes no sense to speak of a given individual as producing or creating an object or state of affairs, then it makes no sense to speak of that individual as having the *ability* to produce a state of affairs. If it is not sensible to speak of an individual as *exercising* a given ability, then it is not sensible to speak of that individual as *having* that ability. A theoretically unexercisable ability is not an ability at all. A timeless being could not only not be omnipotent on the traditional interpretation of 'omnipotent', such a being could have no *creative* ability whatsoever. It is thus not surprising that Schleiermacher would seek an understanding of the notion of omnipotence that does not involve the notion of creative ability.

III

This brings us in for a closer look at the doctrine of divine preservation. Most Christians would probably reject Schleiermacher's 'reductions' of the concept of omnipotence and the concept of creation to the concept of preservation. I think that most Christians would insist that God has power that he does not exercise; and I think that most Christians

Timelessness and Power

would also insist that God's activity with respect to the things that exist involves more than a sustaining activity. God also *produced* the things that He sustains. Still, for the Christian, God does sustain the universe of natural objects. And this idea is related very closely to the idea that God is the omnipotent creator of the natural world. Thus, let's disregard Schleiermacher's 'reductions' of the doctrine of omnipotence and the doctrine of creation. Let's just work with the claim that God sustains or preserves the universe of natural objects.

I think it should be noticed at the outset that there are uses for the verb 'sustains' and its correlative 'depends upon' that do not require that the sustaining or dependent items have temporal extension or temporal location. A valid argument might be described as one in which the premises *sustain* the conclusion. It is also one in which the truth of the conclusion might be described as *depending upon* the truth of the premises. But, it must be remembered that the case we are now considering is one in which it is claimed that a certain individual (usually described as a person) sustains the existence of things such as trees and seas or a complex composed of trees and seas. The things sustained are sustained in the sense that they are made to continue in existence. The relation with which we are working is thus a *material* relation between a person and a set of physical phenomena, not a *logical* relation between propositions or truth values. The question I want to ask is whether this sort of material relation could have a timeless individual as one of its terms.

Imagine a baritone holding middle C for a full minute. Think of this as a single, continuous singing-action that sustains a single, continuous sound. This case is immediately suggested by the model Schleiermacher introduced when dealing with the notion of divine creation, i.e., the 'uttered-thought' model. It is also suggested by Schleiermacher's insistence that the notion of preservation involved in the doctrine of preservation has a productive or 'active' conceptual element. There is a certain productive-energy required in sustaining a sound for a full minute. Now, in order to eliminate the most obvious temporal element in the picture before us, alter the image by allowing both the singing-action and the sound to be indefinitely extended both forward and backward in time. We now have the image of a singing-action that has no beginning and no end. But the action has temporal extension. It is a single, continuous action extended indefinitely both forward and backward in time. The action also has temporal position relative to the sound it sustains. The action is temporally co-extensive with the sound. Let us see if we can modify the image in such a way as to eliminate these remaining temporal features.

Let us suppose that it makes sense to speak of a momentary singing-action (it will not matter for our purposes whether this is really imaginable). This is an action having no duration. Now suppose that an action of this sort results in a sound that goes on forever. We now have the image of a durationless action that bears a material relation to a temporally extended sound. But several temporal ideas still haunt the picture. The action has a beginning and an end. In addition, the action has location in time relative to the beginning of the sound. Further, even if we had failed to notice the temporal elements just mentioned, I doubt that this image would be of any real use in the present discussion. We seem here to be dealing with a case in which the action must be described as *producing*, rather than *sustaining* the sound. Let's try another modification.

Picture a number of momentary singing-actions located at intervals along the history of a single sound. Let the sound and the sequence of actions be indefinitely extended both forward and backward in time. The sequence might be said to sustain the sound in the way in which a number of short-lived breezes sustain the motion of a sailboat. In this image we have only durationless singing-actions and the sequences of actions has no beginning or end. But temporal predicates are still applicable to that which sustains the sound. There is a *sequence* of actions; and each of the actions in the sequence is simultaneous with some part of

Timelessness and Power

the history of the sound. The sequence (though not the individual members of the sequence) also has duration. Let's try one more modification.

Let the sound be indefinitely extended both forward and backward in time. At some point along the way, a single momentary action enters to reinforce the sound. Such an action might be described as sustaining the sound, as a single short-lived breeze sustains the motion of the boat through a certain period of its journey. We have now eliminated the notion of a sequence of actions, and the single action involved has no duration. But time predicates apply to it nonetheless. The action has a beginning and an end. It also occurs simultaneously with some part of the history of the sound.

I can think of no other way of arranging the elements of the baritone image so that it could be described as the image of a singing-action (or group of singing-actions) that sustains a temporally extended sound. With respect to each of the above arrangements, the action (or the group of actions) has temporal extension or, at least, temporal position.

Now let's look at Schleiermacher's description of the preservation relation that obtains between God and the temporally extended universe considered as a unit. R. W. Matthews translates his remarks as follows:[22]

> In the same way, if we regard Preservation as a continuous divine activity exerted on the whole course of the world, covering its first beginnings no less than each subsequent state then this is a complete expression of the self-consciousness in question [the religious consciousness] provided we do not think of the origin of the world as conditioned by something else before or after this activity.

St. Thomas says virtually this same thing about God's preservation activity in Part I of the *Summa Theologica*. He says:[23]

> The conservation of things by God is not a new action, but a continuation of that action whereby He gives being, which action is without either motion or time; so also the conservation of light in the air is by the continual influence of the Sun.

But the image conveyed in these passages is, in essential respects, the one conveyed in the first case of the baritone's creative-sustaining action with respect to the sound of middle C. Schleiermacher says that God's sustaining action is a 'divine activity exerted on the whole course of the world's history covering its first beginnings no less than each subsequent state'. St. Thomas says that this activity is a 'continuation (*continuationem*) of that action whereby He gives being'. This way of talking surely suggests that God's sustaining activity is temporally co-extensive with the duration of the universe – just as in the first image, the baritone's singing-action is temporally co-extensive with the duration of the sound. This point is reinforced by St. Thomas's analogy of the influence of the sun with respect to the light in the air. In this case too, the sustaining action is temporally co-extensive with what is sustained.

We must, then, adjust the description of God's sustaining activity. But how shall we do it? Can we get a description that is, at once, the description of a *sustaining* activity and that does not entail that the activity (and thus the being whose activity it is) has duration or bears some temporal relation to the universe of objects? None of the alternatives mentioned above would suffice; and most of these would be inadequate on other grounds anyway.[24] But perhaps this last point is of limited importance. The alternatives we have just discussed are alternatives with respect to a very special kind of picture. Maybe we need another picture altogether. Let's shift to another way of thinking.

In his presentation and defence of St. Thomas's first argument for the existence of God, Father R. Garrigou-Lagrange writes as follows:[25]

> It may be of help to the imagination to present the proof for the existence of God drawn from motion by taking an example of subordinate causes which appeals to the senses. 'A sailor holds up an anchor on board a ship, the ship supports the sailor, the sea enables the ship to float, the earth holds in check the sea, the sun keeps the earth fixed in its course, and some unknown centre of attraction holds the sun in its place. But after that? ... We cannot

go on in this manner *ad infinitium* in a series of causes that are actually subordinate.' There must be a primary efficient cause which actually exists and gives efficiency to all other causes.

On this account, St. Thomas did not regard God as the first member of a temporally ordered series of causes. God does not cause the universe in the way in which striking a match causes a flame. (This appears to be in line with Schleiermacher's idea that God did not literally *create* or *produce* the universe of natural objects.) According to Garrigou-Lagrange, St. Thomas thought of God as having a place 'above'[26] (or 'below' – i.e., at the ground of) the temporal series. This is the message conveyed in the image of the sailor on the ship. In this picture we are given a series of grounds or supports that are not organized in a temporal sequence. God is the first member of a series of this sort. God supports the universe as the sea supports the ship. Properly speaking, God is not the creator of the universe; He is (as Tillich said) its ground or foundation.

Does this image help with the present problem? I can't see that it does. For one thing, this image seems to have at least one element that makes it even less attractive than the one we were using earlier. The sea supports the ship. But the sea is not active – it doesn't *do* anything. The sea is entirely passive – it is that upon which the ship rests. The same is true as we move from the sea to the earth and from the earth to the sun. What is lacking at each of these intervals in the sequence is the notion of a sustaining *activity*. According to Schleiermacher, the doctrine of divine preservation has productive-overtones – it expresses the 'active' side of God's nature. I think we were better off with the picture of God supporting the universe in the way in which the baritone supports the sound of middle C. But, of course, this observation does not touch the point of central concern. The important difficulty involved in the sailor image is precisely the one involved in the baritone image. The picture makes essential use of a temporal relation between things and their grounds or supports. Could we make sense of the claim that

God and Timelessness

the sea supports the ship if we deleted from our thinking all of the temporal elements in the situation? Try thinking of the sea supporting the ship without thinking of the sea as temporally extended. I can think of no way of modifying the image so as to eliminate this temporal implication.

At this point I should like to consider a possible complaint about procedure. I could imagine someone saying that while the baritone image and the sailor image reveal some aspects of the sustaining relation we are trying to describe, neither accomplishes the whole of the task and both distort the a-temporal nature of God. But after all (the objection continued) these are only pictures. They are intended only to be of 'help to the imagination' (Garrigou-Lagrange). The theory being advanced in no way depends upon the adequacy of such pictures.

I am inclined to think that this complaint has less force than might be expected. In the first place, it is not at all clear that pictures are really dispensable in discussions about the nature of God. We have only the pictures: The being itself is not available for our inspection. Wittgenstein once said that as regards the concept of God, 'The whole *weight* may be in the picture'.[27] The picture seems to be what guides and bolsters the religious life: it is not *just* an aid to the imagination. But secondly, it seems to me that in working with various images (such as the baritone image and the sailor image) we discover something important about our *concept* of the sustaining relation. Begin with the idea that God sustains the universe of natural objects. Now adjust the thinking so as to exclude all temporal elements. This is precisely what St. Thomas invites us to do in the passage cited above. Thomas says that God preserves the universe — he then warns that God's preservation activity is to be conceived of 'without either motion or time'. (I suspect that Thomas felt the need to add this warning because he sensed the clear temporal implications of his claim that God's preservation activity is a *continuation* of His creation-activity.)[28] But it seems to me that this kind of conceptual adjustment is not an adjustment at all – it is a special kind of retraction. In ordinary cases where the preservation relation is clearly identifiable, a temporal relation between that which is preserved and that which does the preserving appears to be an essential part of the relation. I can see no way of eliminating the temporal elements in such cases without eliminating anything that could be counted as a preservation relation. It would thus appear that the temporal elements are not unnecessary sidelights of particular cases. They seem to be at the centre of our thinking about things that sustain or preserve the existence of something else. St. Thomas says that God's preservation activity is 'without either motion or time'. I wonder if this isn't a little like saying that when Gabriel blows his horn, he does it while holding his breath.

Schleiermacher says that the doctrine of God's eternity is incomplete and misleading when considered apart from the notion of His omnipotence. He seems to see that if God is timeless, His omnipotence cannot be understood as the ability to bring things about. He also seems to see that if God is timeless, the standard doctrine of divine creation cannot be accepted. A timeless being could not bring about nor could we have the ability to bring about anything whatsoever. Schleiermacher's position is, then, that God's eternity is incomplete and misleading when considered apart from the concept of God's sustaining activity. The assumption is that this latter concept can be consistently applied when describing the activities of a timeless individual. But, on the surface at least, the relation between the doctrine of divine preservation and the doctrine of timelessness is not one of mutual supplementation. The claim that God preserves the universe of natural objects seems no more compatible with the doctrine of timelessness than does the claim that God produces, or has the ability to produce, temporal states of affairs. Until we are given some further clarification of the idea that God preserves the temporally extended universe of objects, it seems to me that we have

God and Timelessness

the right to suspect that a timeless being could not be the one that performs this particular task.

Postscript I: According to Schleiermacher, both the doctrine of divine creation and the doctrine of divine preservation are expressions of the proposition 'that the totality of finite being exists only in dependence upon the Infinite . . .'[29] We have found reason to think that a timeless being could not create or preserve a temporally extended universe, but this does not show that a timeless individual could not be the one upon which the universe ultimately *depends* for its existence. Consider the following case: Jones and Smith are members of the same family. However, Jones and Smith are not cousins, not brothers, not sisters . . . etc. As long as we do not complete the list of possible family relationships, there is still content in the claim that Jones and Smith are members of the same family. If we were to complete the list, the original claim would be emptied. The same sort of point may be relevant as regards the claim that the universe depends on God. God did not create the universe, God does not preserve the universe, God does not . . . , etc. As long as we do not complete the list of possible dependence relationships, there may still be content in the original claim. It may be that the universe of objects is utterly dependent upon a timeless individual. The problem is to uncover the specific dependence relationship mentioned in this affirmation.

Postscript II: It is interesting to note that the logical tension between the doctrine of God's timelessness on the one hand and the doctrines of omnipotence and creation on the other hand, does not stem from the fact that a timeless being lacks temporal extension (duration). It stems from the fact that a timeless being lacks temporal *position*. At the end of sub-section (*a*), sec. III, Ch. 4, we saw that the lack of temporal *position* is precisely the element in the concept of timelessness that performed the heavy part of the work in Boethius's solution to (or dissolution of) the problem of divine foreknowledge. The claim that God lacks temporal position thus works both to the advantage and to the disadvantage of the systematic theologian.

NOTES

[1] *The Christian Faith.* See the whole of numbered paras. 51–2.
[2] This passage taken from Mackintosh and Stewart, p. 202.
[3] *Summa Theologica*, Pt. 1, Q. 25, A. 3. This passage taken from *The Basic Writings of St. Thomas*, ed. Pegis, New York, Random House, 1954, p. 263.
[4] These verbs are sometimes called 'factitive' verbs.
[5] New York, Robert Appleton Co., 1911.
[6] *The Christian Faith*, numbered para. 54, sec. 3; Mackintosh and Stewart, p. 214.
[7] *Ibid.*, numbered para. 54, sec. 3, pp. 214–15.
[8] *Monologium*, Ch. XX.
[9] *Ibid.*, Ch. XXII. This passage translated by S. N. Deane, *St. Anselm*, La Salle, Open Court, 1958, p. 81.
[10] *The Christian Faith*, numbered para. 40, sec. 1. Mackintosh and Stewart, p. 150.
[11] *Ibid.*, numbered para. 55, sec. 1, p. 221.
[12] *Ibid.*, numbered para. 54, sec. 4, p. 215 ff.
[13] *Ibid.*, numbered para. 54, sec. 1, p. 212.
[14] *Ibid.*, numbered para. 54, sec. 1, p. 212.
[15] See Kant's *First Critique*, 'Second Analogy' (A 203).
[16] *The Christian Faith*, numbered paras. 36–40. See especially Mackintosh and Stewart, pp. 143; 149–51.
[17] *Ibid.*, numbered para. 41, sec. 2, p. 142.
[18] *Ibid.*, numbered para. 41, sec. 2, p. 155.
[19] *Ibid.*, numbered para. 38, pp. 146–8.
[20] *Ibid.*, numbered para. 41, sec. 2, p. 154.
[21] *Ibid.*, numbered para. 36, sec. 1, p. 142.
[22] *Ibid.*, numbered para. 38, sec. 2. The word 'continuous' in the English translation has no direct justification in the German text. In inserting this word, Matthews was obviously trying to capture the *sense* of the passage – the sense that is amply revealed in the rest of the passage.
[23] Q. 104, A. 1, reply to objection 4. This passage is taken from A. C. Pegis, p. 965. See also *Summa Theologica*, P. I, Q. 104, A. 3. Here Thomas says that God does not 'conserve things in being otherwise than by *continually* (*continue*) giving being to them'.
[24] Schleiermacher treats and rejects some of these alternatives in numbered para. 38, sec. 2 of *The Christian Faith*.
[25] *God: His Existence and His Nature*, tr. D. B. Rose, St. Louis, Herder Book Co., 1955, V. I, p. 267.

[26] *Ibid.*, p. 268.

[27] *Lectures and Conversations on Aesthetics, Psychology and Religious Belief*, edited by Cyril Barrett, Berkeley, University Press, 1967, p. 72.

[28] Schleiermacher also keeps reminding us that God's sustaining activity is not to be intepreted as involving a temporal relation between God and the world; see, e.g., numbered paragraph 38, sec. 1 and the postscript of numbered paragraph 46. I strongly suspect that Schleiermacher (like Thomas) is here reacting to an uneasy feeling that he has not really succeeded in describing the preservation relation without making use of temporal implicators.

[29] *The Christian Faith*, numbered para. 36, sec. I, p. 142.

7
God as a Timeless Person

In this chapter I shall examine the notion of timelessness as it relates to the idea of a person. I shall also make a critical comment about the idea of a timeless knower.

I

In his article, 'Professor Malcolm on God', Robert Coburn claims that a timeless being could not qualify as a person. He supports his position as follows: (Keep in mind that Coburn uses 'eternal' to mean 'timeless'.)[1]

> Surely it is a necessary condition of anything's being a person that it should be capable (logically) of, among other things, doing at least some of the following: remembering, anticipating, reflecting, deliberating, deciding, intending, and acting intentionally. To see that this is so, one need only ask oneself whether anything which necessarily lacked all of the capabilities noted would, under any conceivable circumstances, count as a person. But now an eternal being would necessarily lack all of these capacities inasmuch as their exercise by a being clearly requires that the being exist in time. After all, reflection and deliberation takes time; deciding typically occurs at some time—and in any case it always makes sense to ask, 'When did you (he, they, etc,). decide?'; remembering is impossible unless the being doing the remembering has a past; and so on. Hence, an eternal being, it would seem, could not be a person.

Let's look a little more carefully at the mental activities itemized by Coburn. For our purposes, I think we should divide them into three distinct classes.

God and Timelessness

(1) Reflecting and deliberating take time. The individual doing the reflecting or deliberating must then have temporal extension. A timeless being could not reflect or deliberate because a timeless being does not have temporal extension. (Schleiermacher made note of this point).[2]

(2) Anticipating and intending require that the individual doing the anticipating or intending has temporal location. To anticipate something is to think about that thing before it exists or before one learns that it exists (or is true). In similar fashion, to intend something is, at least in part, to think about that thing before it comes about. This last point ties in with a comment made by William Kneale in his article 'Time and Eternity in Theology'. Kneale said that 'to act purposefully is to act with thought of what will come about after the beginning of the action'.[3] (This point connects with Schleiermacher's claim that a timeless being could have no *plans*.)[4] It follows, Coburn says, that a timeless being could neither anticipate nor intend anything. A timeless being could not act purposefully, i.e., intentionally. These arguments rest on an element in the concept of timelessness other than the one operative in the corresponding arguments about reflection and deliberation. Reflection and deliberation take time – they require that the agent have temporal *extension*. But with respect to anticipation and intention, the problem is not that these activities require an agent having temporal extension, it is, rather, that they require an agent having temporal *position* relative to the things anticipated or intended. (Coburn includes decision-making in this second category of activities.)

(3) To remember is to think about something after one has experienced it or learned about it. Thus, if one is to remember something, one must have position in time. A timeless individual could not remember. The argument leading to this conclusion is parallel with the one just given with respect to anticipating and intending. It rests on the fact that a timeless individual lacks temporal position. But, further, an individual can remember only what *he* has experienced or learned in the past. We thus have a *second*

reason for saying that a timeless individual could not remember. The argument here is not parallel with the one given with respect to anticipating and intention – since it is aimed at showing that remembering requires an agent having temporal extension rather than temporal position. This argument is also to be distinguished from the argument supporting the claim that a timeless individual could not reflect or deliberate. In the case of reflection and deliberation, the activity takes time and thus requires an agent having temporal extension. But in the case of remembering, even if the activity itself did not take time, the individual engaged in remembering would have to have duration. A man can remember only what *he* has experienced or learned in the past. He must then have a past. This is the rationale of the second argument for the claim that a timeless individual could not remember.

Up to this point, it seems to me that Coburn's argument is in good order. What we have learned is that a timeless individual would be in principle incapable of engaging in a number of important mental activities. But Coburn now concludes that a timeless being could not be described as a person. In order to count as a person, he says, an individual must be able to perform at least some of the mental activities mentioned. I think that this conclusion is premature.

For Coburn, the centre of the concept of a person seems to be located in the idea of mental ability. When discussing the concept of a person, his attention is focused entirely on mental powers such as the ability to deliberate, anticipate and remember. But if this is the right approach to the concept of a person, it would seem that if a timeless individual could be omniscient (i.e., if a timeless being could have unlimited knowledge), that would be enough to assure that such a being might count as a person even if it could not deliberate, anticipate or remember. To be sure, squirrels, e.g., have knowledge (I suppose) and they are not persons. But we are here dealing with the idea of an individual having complete and perfect knowledge. Such an individual would surely have unmatched stature among intellectual beings. I should think that if a given individual could be described as omniscient, that would be sufficient grounds for the claim that the individual in question is a person.

Could any of the three patterns of argument just reviewed in connection with deliberation, anticipation and memory be applied in the case of knowledge?

To deliberate is to do something. If I deliberate about going to the park, I think about going to the park – weighing the pros and cons one after the other. Any activity not involving this sequential outlay of mental energy could not be counted as a case of deliberation. This is why Coburn could say with confidence that deliberation takes time. But I can't see that this same sort of point could be made as regards knowledge. The knowing-state does not appear to be a state of mental action. It is not at all clear that knowing is a kind of doing. What is he doing? . . . He is deliberating. That makes sense. What is he doing? . . . He is knowing. That makes no sense at all. One might say that in order to know something one must think about it. Thinking about something (so it might be urged) is a kind of doing that takes time. But I don't think that one *must* say this. It is not clear that one must think about something (where 'think' marks an activity taking time) in order to be described as knowing something.

To anticipate, intend or remember something requires that one think about that thing at a time either before or after the thing occurs or exists, or at a time either before or after one learns that it occurs, exists or is true. But, again, I can't see that the same sort of point could be made with respect to knowledge. 'x knows that ϕ' does not entail that x (or his knowledge) exists before ϕ, that x (or his knowledge) exists after ϕ, that x (or his knowledge) occurs simultaneously with ϕ. (I made this same point in the first chapter with respect to God's *awareness* of ϕ.). Further, 'x knows that ϕ' does not seem to entail the existence of a temporal relation between x (or his knowledge) and x's *learning* that ϕ. This is so, I think, because 'x knows that ϕ' does not entail 'x learned that ϕ'. One can know things one has not learned. I know that my eyes are now open, but this is not something I learned.

The third pattern of argument used by Coburn (the one that provides the second reason for thinking that a timeless individual could not remember) has no application in the present discussion. I don't think that knowing requires (logically) that one has learned or experienced something in the past.

So far as I can see, nothing that Coburn has said, or suggested, shows that a timeless individual could not have knowledge. But if a timeless individual could have knowledge – at least if it could have unlimited knowledge – then we could at least conceive of the case in which a timeless individual would have to be counted as a person. This is true if it is also true that a timeless individual could not deliberate, anticipate or remember.

II

Let us inquire about the conditions under which we would say that John knows (or even believes) that there is, e.g., an apple in the barrel. John might speak, saying: 'There is an apple in the barrel.' On the other hand, John might walk to the barrel and pick out the apple; John might write a letter to a friend describing the apple in the barrel; John might place a bet on there being an apple in the barrel, and so on. Now, a timeless being is, of necessity, incorporeal (Ch. 3). But an incorporeal being could not speak as opposed to, say, emit sounds. In order to speak, one must have a mouth or something like a mouth. (Peter Lombard made this point in the *Sentences*: I, d. 42, Ch. 2.) For similar reasons, an incorporeal being could not walk to the barrel and reach for the apple nor could it write a letter to a friend describing the apple in the barrel. In order to walk, one must have legs or something like legs; and in order to write a letter, one must hold a pencil in one's hand, make a typewriter go with one's fingers, or dictate (speak) to another who writes it down on paper. The same holds for betting. To bet, one must speak (saying, e.g., 'I bet', 'You're on', etc.), or one must nod one's head, wave one's money in the air, etc. It would appear that the kinds of things one must do before we would have warrant for saying that he knows or believes something are not the kinds of things that could be done by an incorporeal being. It follows, of course, that the sorts of things one must do before we would have warrant for saying that he knows something are not the kinds of things that could be done by a timeless being.

However, I think that this argument is deficient. Let us suppose that we know there to be an incorporeal being in the room. It will not matter for our purposes how we came to have this information. In the course of conversation, I assert: 'There is no apple in the barrel.' We hear a voice say: 'Yes there is.' I challenge the statement. In response to my challenge we hear the voice say: 'Put up your money.' We see a five dollar bill waving vigorously in the air and come to rest on the table. A moment later we see the apple rising slowly from the barrel. The voice says: 'I told you so.' Given enough data of this sort, I think we might eventually have to admit that the incorporeal being knew (or at least believed) that there was an apple in the barrel. We might hesitate to say that he had spoken to us or that he had walked to the barrel and picked up the apple. But someone might suggest that while the incorporeal being did not speak, he brought it about that a voice was heard. While the incorporeal being did not pick up the apple, he brought it about that the apple arose from the barrel. In so far as we could regard the data as having been *produced* or *brought about* by the incorporeal being, we could receive the data as evidence that he knew (or believed) there to be an apple in the barrel. It would thus appear that under certain very extravagant conditions, we might have warrant for saying that an incorporeal being knew (or believed) something. The key to the matter rests in the idea that an incorporeal being might be able to bring about circumstances which, if brought about in the usual way by an ordinary individual, would give warrant for saying that the individual in question knew (or believed) something.

I doubt that this general line of thinking is going to be of any use as regards a timeless being. There is reason to think that a timeless being could not bring about circumstances of the sort we are considering. This is because there is reason to think that a timeless being could bring about nothing whatsoever (Ch. 7). We seem to be approaching the view that under no conditions would we have warrant for saying that a timeless being has knowledge or holds beliefs.

Let us agree that there exists a timeless being. Could this individual know, believe, be aware of, 'behold', 'see', etc., things? The trouble here is not that 'x knows that ϕ' and 'x is aware of ϕ' are subject to the kinds of observations made above with respect to anticipation, deliberation and the like. It is not that knowing takes time or that knowing requires that there be a temporal relation between the knower and what he knows. The trouble is that a timeless being could not *act* in the various ways demanded of one who would qualify as knowing, believing or being aware of something. Shall we then say that it is *meaningless* to speak of a timeless being as having knowledge or as being aware of something? I'm not sure that this is the right conclusion. After all, theologians such as Boethius and Schleiermacher have claimed to find a meaningful residue in the notion of the timeless and omniscient being – even though in this case 'knows' and 'is aware of' have been stripped of their normal ties with behaviour. Still, it seems to me that we are due something in the way of an explanation. What we need are meaning-directions – perhaps, *picturing*-directions. We need some way of understanding what the difference would be between a timeless being that does *not* have knowledge (e.g., the number two) and a timeless being that does have knowledge. Until we have this, I think we have an obligation to be reluctant about whether we really understand the idea of a timeless knower.

God and Timelessness

III

A timeless being could not deliberate, anticipate, or remember. It could not speak or write a letter, nor could it produce sounds or written words on a piece of paper. It could not smile, grimace or weep. Further, a timeless being could not be affected or prompted by another. It could not respond to needs, overtures, delights or antagonisms of human beings. There are two distinct issues connected with this last point: (1) A timeless being is immutable in the strong sense of 'immutable' (Ch. 3). Such an individual could not be affected or prompted by another. To be affected or prompted by another is to be changed by the other. (2) The actions of a timeless being could not be interpreted as a *response* to something else. Responses are located in time *after* that to which they are responses. In addition to this list of inabilities, there now appears to be a conceptual difficulty involved in the idea of a timeless knower. It is not at all clear that we really understand what it would be for a timeless being to know, believe or be aware of something. At this point, I think we should adopt the position set out by Coburn. An individual that is (in principle) incapable of all of these things could not be counted as a person.

There is one more point to be made in this connection.

Let us agree for the moment that given some as yet unimagined circumstance, a timeless being might have to be counted as a person. What kind of a person would it be? An individual incapable of the range of performances just listed would surely not rank very high on the personality scale. I doubt if one could become emotionally involved with such a person. I don't think one could take him as a friend – or as an enemy. Further, I don't think that a timeless person could be emotionally involved with another. To be emotionally involved, one must be able to *respond* in some way to the actions or inactions of others. A timeless individual could not respond. Thus, even if we could imagine circumstances under which a timeless individual could be counted as a person (and I doubt that we could), the question would still remain: How much of a person would a timeless person be?

NOTES

[1] *Australasian Journal of Philosophy*, v. 40–1, J (1962–3), p. 155.
[2] *The Christian Faith*, numbered para. 55, sec. 2.
[3] 'Time and Eternity in Theology', *Proceedings of the Aristotelian Society*, 1961, p. 99.
[4] *The Christian Faith*, numbered para. 41, sec. 1.

8
The Justification of the Doctrine of Timelessness: Anselm

St. Anselm said that God is a being a greater than which cannot be conceived. God is an absolutely perfect being. In the second chapter of the *Proslogium* Anselm says (in effect) that this formula articulates 'our concept', i.e., the Christian (or, as he suggests in the fifth chapter of the *Responsio*, the 'Catholic') concept of God. Further, according to Anselm, if God is a being a greater than which cannot be conceived, then God is eternal, immutable, omnipotent, omniscient, perfectly benevolent and so on for each of the attributes usually assigned to God in the Christian tradition. 'God is a being a greater than which cannot be conceived' *entails* 'God is eternal', 'God is immutable', 'God is omnipotent', and the like. Of course, Anselm interpreted the predicate 'eternal' to mean 'timeless'. He thus intended that the formula expressing the centre of our concept of God should entail 'God is timeless'. In this chapter I shall examine this last mentioned thesis. I shall argue that it is not at all clear that the doctrine of God's timelessness can be justified by reference to a logical connection between 'God is a being a greater than which cannot be conceived' and 'God is timeless'.

Unfortunately, Anslem did very little to explicate the precise import of the statement 'God is a being a greater than which cannot be conceived'. In particular, he did not make clear how this formula is supposed to entail propositions

The Justification of the Doctrine of Timelessness: Anselm

such as 'God is eternal', 'God is immutable', 'God is omnipotent', etc. He thus did not spell out the details of his procedure for justifying propositions about the nature of God. Very early in my deliberations on this topic I discovered that I could not avoid confronting this difficulty. In what is to follow, I shall spend what might seem to be a disproportionate amount of time developing an interpretation of Anselm's justification-procedure. It is my hope that the reader will be patient with me on this score. The matter is more complicated than one might be inclined to think.

I

It will be important at a later stage in our investigation that we recognize a difference in meaning between the statement 'God is a being a greater than which cannot be conceived' and the statement 'God is the greatest of all beings'. In anticipation of this later need, I should like to begin this study with a consideration of the following passage from Norman Malcolm's article 'Anselm's Ontological Arguments':[1]

> ... there is certainly *a* use of 'God', and I think far the most common use, in accordance with which the statement 'God is the greatest of all beings', 'God is the most perfect being' and 'God is the supreme being', are logically necessary truths, in the same sense that the statement, 'squares have four sides' is a logically necessary truth. If there is a man named 'Jones' who is the tallest man in the world, the statement 'Jones is the tallest man in the world' is merely true and is not a logically necessary truth. It is a virtue of Anselm's unusual phrase 'a being a greater than which cannot be conceived', to make explicit that the sentence 'God is the greatest of all beings' expresses a logically necessary truth and not a mere matter of fact such as the one we just imagined about Jones.

Malcolm says that the point of the formula 'God is a being a greater than which cannot be conceived' is to make explicit that the statements, 'God is the greatest of all beings', 'God is the supreme being', and 'God is the most perfect being', express logically necessary truths. There seem to me to be

God and Timelessness

two reasons for thinking that Anselm's formula ought not to be read in this way.

First, Anselm would probably deny that, 'God is the greatest of all beings' and 'God is the supreme being', are logically necessary truths. In the fifteenth chapter of the *Monologium*, Anselm says that the terms 'greatest' and 'supreme' are 'relative expressions'. By this he means that these terms apply to a given individual only if that individual compares with (is related to) other things in a certain way. An individual could not be the greatest of all beings if it existed alone in the world any more than a man could be the tallest of all men if he were the only man in existence. Now, given this observation, we know that if God exists and if God is the greatest of all beings, something other than God exists. Together, 'God exists' and 'God is the greatest of all beings' *entail* 'Something other than God exists'. But the statement, 'Something other than God exists' must surely be counted as a contingent statement. It follows that if 'God is the greatest of all beings' is a necessary statement (as Malcolm says), then 'God exists' must be a contingent statement. There must be at least one contingent proposition in any set of p opositions that entails a contingent proposition. In this cas , if it is not 'God is the greatest of all beings' that is contingent, it must be 'God exists'. Of course, Anselm held that 'God exists' is a necessary statement. This was an essential part of his strategy for proving the existence of God. Thus Anselm would have to deny that 'God is the greatest of all beings' is a logically necessary truth. Precisely this same reasoning would require that Anselm reject 'God is the supreme being', 'God is the creator of the universe', 'God exercises providence over all things', etc., as ogically necessary truths. In each of these cases a predicate is assigned to God that relates Him to other things. These propositions could be true only if something other than God exists. But if it is contingent that things other than God exist, then these could be necessary truths only if 'God exists' is a contingent proposition. To be sure, Anselm could agree (and, indeed, would agree) that 'God is the

The Justification of the Doctrine of Timelessness: Anselm

greatest of all beings', 'God is the supreme being', 'God is the creator of the universe', etc., are *true* statements. His claim that 'God exists' is a necessary truth requires only that he not assign them the status of *necessary* truths.

Secondly, even if we were to admit that 'God is the greatest of all beings', and 'God is the supreme being' are necessary truths, this is not the message conveyed in the formula 'God is a being a greater than which cannot be conceived'. The argument for this claim requires the following two preliminary observations.

(1) The statement 'God is a being a greater than which cannot be conceived' does not entail 'God is the greatest of all beings'. Let us suppose that omnipotence, immutability, perfect benevolence, etc., are value-making features of things. Let us also suppose that a being is greater or lesser depending on the number of these properties it possesses. Now consider a being possessing *all* of these qualities. Such a being would be logically incapable of improvement – it would be a being a greater than which cannot be conceived. But this being might not be the greatest of all beings. It would not be the greatest of all beings if, for example, it existed by itself in the world. In this situation, the 'relative' predicates 'greatest' and 'supreme' would not be applicable though the being in question would be a greater than which cannot be conceived.

(2) The statement 'God is the greatest of all beings' does not entail 'God is a being a greater than which cannot be conceived'. Again, let us suppose that omnipotence, immutability, perfect benevolence, etc., are value-making features of things and that a being is greater or lesser depending on the number of these qualities it possesses. Now consider a universe containing just three individuals. The first of these is immutable and perfectly good, while the second and third are immutable but not perfectly good. All three are alike in other respects. No one of the three is omnipotent. If we assume that it is logically possible for all of the value-making features to characterize one being, in this situation the first of these individuals would count as the

greatest of all beings (i.e., the supreme being), but it would not be a being a greater than which cannot be conceived. To be a being a greater than which cannot be conceived, it would have to possess *all* of the value-making features of objects and thus would have to be omnipotent as well as immutable, perfectly benevolent, and the like. Even if the first being were the greatest of all beings, we could *conceive* of a being greater than it, *viz.*, one just like it except for being omnipotent as well as immutable, perfectly benevolent, etc. I think that this was the point Anselm was making in the fifth chapter of the *Responsio* when he criticized Guanilo for reading 'God is a being a greater than which cannot be conceived' as 'God is the greatest of all beings'. From what he says in this passage, Anselm seems to have seen very clearly that a being might be the greatest of all beings without possessing all of the value-making features of things.

We now have enough to proceed to the following two conclusions: first, 'God is a being a greater than which cannot be conceived' does not entail '"God is the greatest of all beings" is a necessary truth'. We could imagine a universe in which God exists and the first of these statements is true but in which 'God is the greatest of all beings' is not only not a necessary truth but is, in fact, false. This would be a universe containing a being possessing all of the value-making features of things; but a universe having no other members. Second, ' "God is the greatest of all beings" is a necessary truth' does not entail 'God is a being a greater than which cannot be conceived'. Let us suppose that 'God is the greatest of all beings' is a necessary truth. In a universe containing only imperfect beings the greatest of the lot might bear the title 'God' though it would not be a being a greater than which cannot be conceived. In this situation, if a being greater than the ones already existing were suddenly to come into existence, it would displace the one formerly holding the title 'God': 'God is the greatest of all beings' is a necessary truth. But if these conclusions are right, I think we must dismiss Malcolm's claim that 'God is a being a

The Justification of the Doctrine of Timelessness: Anselm

greater than which cannot be conceived' is a way of making explicit: ' "God is the greatest of all beings" is a necessary truth'. These two statements are logically independent (neither entails nor is entailed by the other). Thus, they could not be alternative ways of saying the same thing. If they were ways of saying the same thing, they would have the same meaning: and propositions having the same meaning are not logically independent.

II

Anselm said that each of the qualities possessed by God is such that '... if taken independently, *to be it* is better than *not to be it*'.[2] Such qualities are usually referred to as divine 'perfections'. In this section I shall attempt to clarify some of the general features of qualities fitting into the class.

Consider the following game: There are two doors. Behind each door is an object. On the front of each door is written the name of a quality. On the second door is written the contradictory of the name written on the first. So, for example, if 'red' is written on the first door, 'not-red' will be written on the second. You are given the following information. The object behind each of the doors bears the quality indicated on the front. (For purposes of this discussion the concept of a quality will be stretched just a bit. 'Not-red', for example, will be counted as the name of a quality.) Further, the object behind one of the doors is such that it ought to be preserved. You are to choose a door. The point of the game is to pick the door concealing the object that ought to be preserved. You are to use only the information given on the front of the door. You are not to speculate or guess about the other features of the objects behind the doors.

I'll start the game by writing 'red' on the first door and 'not-red' on the second. I think there is no right choice in this case. Neither the quality red nor the quality not-red is itself a value-making feature of objects. The fact that one object is red and the other object is not-red does not provide

God and Timelessness

a reason for thinking that one or the other of them ought to be preserved.

Now write 'conscious' on the first door and 'not-conscious' on the second door. Let the term 'conscious' apply to any being that either is, or is capable of being aware – even if at a given moment, that being is unconscious or asleep. Here, the door marked 'conscious' would appear to be the right choice. If something is alive and conscious, that is a reason for preserving it. Consider the following exchange: A small boy drops a live frog in his mother's pulverizer. Father reprimands him: 'You ought not to have done that.' The boy calls for an explanation. Father replies: 'That was a living, conscious thing.' Father's reply may not be conclusive – there may be overriding reasons for destroying the frog. But father's reply is at least relevant as backing for his reprimand. That the frog was a living, conscious being is a good reason for not destroying it. Now consider the parallel exchange for the quality non-conscious. The boy drops his mother's watch in the pulverizer. Father reprimands him: 'You ought not to have done that.' The boy calls for an explanation. Father replies: 'That was a non-conscious thing.' This reply is absurd. That the watch was useful, beautiful, his mother's favourite, etc., would be relevant things to mention when grounding the reprimand, but the quality non-conscious is not a value-making feature of things. It is not a feature that makes a thing such that it ought to be preserved. Thus, given only that the object behind the first door is conscious and the object behind the second door is not conscious, there is reason to think that it is the object behind the first door that ought to be preserved. There is no similar reason for thinking that it is the object behind the second door that ought to be preserved. This is why the right choice in this case is the first door.

I have constructed the two-door game in order to provide a graphic way of isolating three important features of the qualities that are to be counted as 'perfections'. The first two of these features are brought out by Anselm in the following passage from the *Monologium*:[3]

The Justification of the Doctrine of Timelessness: Anselm

... to be wise is better than not to be so; that is, it is better to be wise than not to be wise. For, though one who is just but not wise, is apparently a better man than one who is wise but not just, yet, taken by itself, it is not better *not to be wise* than *to be wise*. For everything that is not wise, simply in so far as it is not wise, is less than what is wise, since everything that is not wise would be better if it were wise.

In this passage it is made clear that a value-making feature of a thing is a feature the possession of which makes the thing better than it would otherwise be. Anselm emphasizes, however, that in order to detect the value-making import of a given quality, one must consider that quality and its contradictory *by themselves* – in isolation of any other qualities a given object might have. This ties in with a prominent feature of the two-door game. The rules of the game require that we consider a given quality and its contradictory *by themselves*, apart from any consideration of other features the objects behind the doors may have. The rules of the game neutralize all other features by barring them from consideration. What we discover when we discover that it would be wrong to choose the door marked 'non-conscious' is that *all other things being equal*, a conscious being is more valuable than a non-conscious being.

Secondly, Anselm makes clear in this passage that it is not required of a value-making feature that everything that has it be better than everything that lacks it. Wisdom is a value-making feature of men. All other things being equal, the man who is wise is better than the man who is not wise. But a man who is wise might not be as good as a man who is not wise. This would be true if the first man were wise but not just and the second man were just but not wise. This point might be extended. A man who is wise and, e.g., cruel is a better man than he would be if he were not wise and cruel, even though a man who is not wise and not cruel might be a better man than one who is wise and cruel. In our game, working with the qualities conscious and non-conscious, we discovered that the quality conscious is a value-making characteristic. But this does not mean that all conscious

God and Timelessness

things are better than all non-conscious things. Compare the *Mona Lisa* with a frog. Of the two, the *Mona Lisa* is probably more valuable even though the frog is a conscious being and the *Mona Lisa* is not. What the game allows us to see about this case is that in so far as the *Mona Lisa* is not conscious, it lacks a value-making feature possessed by the frog. If it is more valuable than the frog, it is so by virtue of *other features* which it possesses and the frog lacks. *On balance*, the *Mona Lisa* is more valuable than the frog. But this is consistent with the claim that the frog has a value-making feature that the *Mona Lisa* does not have. Considered by itself, to be conscious is better than not to be conscious – but some non-conscious things may be better than some conscious things.

I think I can best get at the third feature of a 'perfection' to which I should like to draw attention, by examining an argument of Norman Malcolm's that seems to me to contain a subtle mistake. Malcolm is trying to show that *independence* is a 'perfection' and thus that it would have to be possessed by the being a greater than which cannot be conceived. He argues as follows:[4]

> If a housewife has a set of extremely fragile dishes, then as dishes, they are inferior to those of another set like them in all respects except that they are not fragile. Those of the first set are *dependent* for their continued existence on gentle handling; those of the second set are not. There is a definite connection in ordinary language between the notions of dependency and inferiority and independence and superiority... Correlative with the notions of dependency and independence are the notions of limited and unlimited. An engine requires fuel and this is a limitation. An engine that could accomplish the same work in the same time and was in all respects satisfactory but did not require fuel would be a superior engine.

Malcolm says that there is a conceptual connection between the notions of dependence and inferiority on the one hand and between the notions of independence and superiority on the other. The move to support this claim begins by asking us to consider two sets of dishes which are alike in every respect except that the dishes making up the first set are

The Justification of the Doctrine of Timelessness: Anselm

fragile while the dishes making up the second set are non-fragile. We are here trying to determine the value-making import of the quality non-fragile. Thus Malcolm (rightly) starts by neutralizing all features of dishes other than non-fragile and its contradictory, fragile. We are then reminded of the clear advantages the housewife enjoys if she uses non-fragile dishes rather than fragile dishes. The conclusion is that non-fragile dishes (i.e., independent dishes) are better dishes than fragile dishes. A similar argument is used to show that independence from a fuel supply is a value-making feature of engines considered as engines.

Consider the man who runs a side-show in the carnival. People get prizes for breaking dishes with baseballs. A salesman presents him with two types of dishes — alike in all respects except that one type is breakable and the other is non-breakable. If he were to choose the non-breakable type, no one would play his game and he would go out of business. Being unbreakable is not a value-making feature of side-show dishes whatever may be true of the dishes used by the housewife. Again: Jones makes fire-alarm boxes for the city of Los Angeles. A salesman presents him with two types of window glass — alike in all respects except that one type is breakable and the other is not. If Jones were to use unbreakable glass in the window of the fire-alarm boxes, no one could turn in a fire alarm. He chooses the breakable glass for obvious reasons. With respect to fire-alarm window glass, unbreakable is not a value-making feature whatever might be true of window glass used for windows in houses or windows in cockpits of fighter planes. Once more: Jones runs a testing service for gasoline companies. He maintains a set of engines by which he measures the relative effectiveness of various gasoline mixtures. A salesman presents him with two types of engines — alike in every respect except that one type uses fuel and the other type does not. An engine that uses no fuel would be of no use in Jones's business. Independence from a fuel supply is not a value-making feature of test engines whatever might be true of the engine used in the family automobile. The point is that we cannot say categorically that independence is a value-making feature with respect to every type of thing considered as the type it is. We can't even say that independence is a value-making feature of every type of dish or every type of engine considered as the type it is.

How then shall we understand the claim that there is a conceptual connection between the notions of dependence and inferiority and between the notions of independence and superiority? St. Anselm gives us a clue in the following remarks about the quality golden:[5]

> But in some cases, *not to be* a certain thing is better than *to be it*, as *not to be gold* may be better than *to be gold*. For it is better for man not to be gold, than to be gold; although it might be better for something to be gold than not to be gold – lead, for instance. For though both, namely, man and lead are not gold, man is something as much better than gold, as he would be of inferior nature, were he gold; while lead is something as much more base than gold, as it would be more precious, were it gold.

If we look only at what Anselm says here about gold and man, it might appear that the point is, simply, that being made of gold is not a value-characteristic of men considered *as men*. Golden men are not better *men* than non-golden men. But what Anselm says in this passage about gold and lead requires a very different reading. Anselm is not saying that being made of gold is a value-characteristic of lead considered *as lead*. If something were made of gold it would not be a better *leaden* thing than something not made of gold. The point has to be (and, indeed this is confirmed in the second half of the passage) that golden things are better *things* than leaden things and that human beings are better *things* than golden things. We are working on a level of abstraction where we consider things (dishes, engines, golden objects, human beings, etc.) as *things* not as the specific kinds of things they are.

If there is a conceptual connection between the notions of independence and superiority and between the notions of dependence and inferiority I think we can see where it will have to be located. The independent dish may be no better

The Justification of the Doctrine of Timelessness: Anselm

dish than the dependent dish. But the independent dish may be a better *object* than the dependent dish. The independent side-show dish is an inferior side-show dish relative to the dependent side-show dish. But the independent side-show dish may be a better *object* than the dependent side-show dish. Inferior objects are sometimes better suited to certain purposes than superior objects.

I think it must be admitted that the kind of value-judgement that we are here encountering is very difficult to understand. At a dog show, the judge rules that this beagle is a better beagle than that beagle. At the end of the show he is asked to make cross-type judgements, e.g., he is asked to decide whether this beagle is a better *dog* than that spaniel. But no one would ask the judge at a dog show to decide whether this beagle is a better *object* than, e.g., a kitchen dish. How could such a judgement be made? Yet, this sort of judgement is regularly made by us in everyday life. A dog-lover judges that his dog is a more valuable object than a kitchen dish – he spends his money on his dog and eats from a tin plate. If the house is burning down, he saves the dog and pays no attention to the dish. This is so even if the commercial value of the dog is considerably less than the commercial value of the dish. Consider the case where it is one's child in the burning house. One judges that the child is better (more valuable) than the dish. This is not to say that the child is a better *child* than the dish – the dish is not a contestant in that competition.

Our two-door game provides a context in which we are forced to make value judgements of this kind. We are not told what kinds of objects are behind the doors – dishes, engines, children, etc. The game requires that we consider the object as objects. Our judgements do not concern the relative place of objects within a given species. Thus, for example, in our first turn with the two-door game we discovered that the property of being conscious is a value-making feature of objects considered as objects. It does not follow, however, that the property of being conscious is a value-making feature of objects considered *as dishes* or *engines*. Which is the better dish — a conscious dish or a non-conscious dish? The question is not intelligible. And even if we managed to import some kind of picture-meaning into the question, the answer would appear to be: the non-conscious dish. A conscious dish (if that makes sense) would probably have trouble with hot foods and soapy water. Still, it might be that the conscious dish would be a more valuable *object* than the non-conscious dish even if the property of being conscious is not a value-making feature of dishes considered as dishes. The property of being conscious may be a value-making feature of objects, considered as objects, whether or not it is a value-making feature of objects considered as the *kinds* of objects they are.

The feature of a perfection that I have just tried to isolate has special significance as regards the problem of picking out the attributes traditionally assigned to God. In Anselm's formula, God is described as a *being* (i.e., a thing) a greater than which cannot be conceived. God is not the best conceivable dish nor the best conceivable engine. He is not the best of some special kind of other thing. God is the best conceivable *being*. Accordingly, God must have all of those features that make objects better objects — not necessarily those features that make dishes better dishes or engines better engines. There may be features which make dishes better dishes but which are not attributes of God — being flat, for example. There may also be features possessed by God that would not make dishes better dishes, e.g., being conscious. The two-door game is set up in such a way as to ensure that we consider attributes from the point of view of their value-making import for beings or objects. It thus provides a guarantee that we do not get sidetracked with Malcolm into irrelevant considerations about features that make objects of certain kinds better objects of their kind.

III

God is a being a greater than which cannot be conceived. Anselm concludes that God is eternal, immutable, perfectly

The Justification of the Doctrine of Timelessness: Anselm

benevolent, perfectly just, etc. Clearly the centre of the inference involved in this two-step sequence is the value-concept operating in the premise – the one expressed by 'greater' in the phrase 'a greater than which cannot be conceived'. I now want to direct attention to the problem of interpreting this value-concept. In this third section of the present chapter, I shall attempt to clarify some of the procedural issues that arise in connection with this problem. In the section following this one, I shall examine a specific interpretation of 'greater' that has been proposed in the contemporary literature on Anselm's theology.

(*a*) John Stuart Mill said (roughly) that propositions of the form 'A is right' mean 'A produces (or preserves) good'. Mill used the value-concept (good) as a primitive when analysing the ethical-concept (right). In the two-door game discussed in the last section, this procedure was reversed. Our question about the relative value of the objects behind the doors was framed by asking: 'Which of the two objects *ought to be preserved?*' In effect, we were identifying a sense of 'good' (i.e., 'valuable') that is analysable in terms of the ethical concept 'ought to be preserved'. I am now going to apply this value-concept as a practice interpretation of the term 'greater' in the phrase 'greater than which cannot be conceived'. I call this a 'practice interpretation' because it is not intended as a serious analysis of the value notion working in Anselm's formula. As we shall see below, if entertained as a serious analysis, it would most certainly fail – it would not meet the criteria of adequacy by which any such analysis must be measured. I employ it here only as part of a preliminary investigation of the methodological issues involved in the topic now under consideration.

Let us suppose that God is a being a *more worthy of preservation* than which cannot be conceived. What specific features could be attributed to God if we knew that this formula described his nature?

Assume that it is logically possible for all value-making

features of objects to attach to the same individual. We might call this 'Leibniz's principle', since it was Leibniz who first identified this assumption as essential to the procedure used by Anselm for justifying statements in which attributes are assigned to God. Given this assumption, we could infer that God is a conscious being rather than a non-conscious being. The reasoning is as follows: The two-door game reveals that the property of being conscious is a value-making feature of objects considered as objects. Now, of course, if we knew only that God is valuable – or even that He is the most valuable thing in the world – we could *not* infer that God is a conscious being. Though the property of being conscious is a value-making feature of objects, it is possible that something not having this quality could be the most valuable thing in the world. As Anselm pointed out in his discussion of the just man and the wise man, this would be possible even if we knew there to be conscious individuals in the world. (This is the point I was emphasizing when I criticized Malcolm in the first section of this chapter.) However, if it is possible for all value-making features of objects to characterize the same object (Leibniz's principle), then if God is a being a more worthy of preservation than which cannot be conceived, God would have to possess *all* of the value-making features of things and thus would have to be a conscious individual. For any being (x) lacking the feature of consciousness, there might not *be* an object more valuable than x, but we could *conceive* of a being more valuable than x, *viz.*, one just like x except for being conscious. The two-door game provides an aid to intuition when picking out the value-making features of objects. It thus provides a tool by which to detect the logical implications of Anselm's formula given our practice interpretation of 'greater'.

What other features might be derived in this way? This question sends us back to the two-door game. Write 'person' on the first door and 'not-person' on the second. The door marked 'person' would appear to be the right choice. The argument: 'This object ought to be preserved because it is a person' is intelligible—indeed, it is a strong argument.

The Justification of the Doctrine of Timelessness: Anselm

By contrast: 'This object ought to be preserved because it is not a person' is not intelligible. One by one, write 'intelligent', 'knowledgeable' and 'wise' on the first door and their contradictories on the second. Again, in each case, the first door would appear to be the right choice. The same seems to be true of the so-called 'moral qualities' usually assigned to God. Write 'benevolent', 'merciful', and 'just' on the first door and their contradictories on the second. Again, the choice seems clear. All of these seem to be value-making features of things considered as things. They would thus have to be chosen given the rules of the game we are playing. By the same argument pattern used above when dealing with the predicate 'conscious', we can now conclude that 'God is a being a greater than which cannot be conceived' entails 'God is a person', 'God is knowledgeable', 'God is benevolent', etc.

Now let's make a second assumption. In the Introduction of this essay I described what I called the 'exemplary version' of a given quality as being that quality devoid of the defects that attend it in the usual case. Let us suppose, for example, that incompleteness, the fact that it is gained *via* a process of learning and the fact that it is discursive are 'defects' of knowledge in the normal case, i.e., are 'defects' of the knowledge possessed by Socrates. Of course, I do not mean to suggest that I really understand how to identify 'defects' of knowledge in the normal case, but let us imagine that this list is accurate. The exemplary version of knowledge would then be knowledge free of these features. Our second assumption is this: All other things being equal, an object is better or worse depending on how closely its value-making characteristics approximate to their exemplary versions. All other things being equal, if A is more knowledgeable than B, then A is better than B, i.e., A ought to be preserved over B. This is so because if A has more knowledge than B, then A's knowledge is more complete than B's and thus A's knowledge approaches more nearly to the exemplary version of knowledge than does B's. It now follows that for any given value-making characteristic of objects, a being more worthy of preservation than which cannot be conceived would have to possess the exemplary version of that characteristic. If a given individual did not possess the exemplary version of a given value-making feature, there might not *be* an object more valuable than it, but we could *conceive* of an object more valuable than it, *viz.*, one just like it except for having the exemplary version of the feature in question. Given the two assumptions made explicit above, as presently interpreted, Anselm's formula entails not only, e.g., 'God is knowledgeable', but also 'God is omniscient' – where 'omniscient' names the exemplary version of knowledge, i.e., perfect knowledge.

(*b*) At this point it would appear that our practice interpretation of 'greater' in the formula 'God is a being a greater than which cannot be conceived' renders the formula such as to imply precisely the propositions about the nature of God that Anselm would readily endorse. However, this appearance is deceptive and it is important for our investigation that we see that this is so.

Write 'powerful' on the first door and 'not-powerful' on the second door. I think that these alternatives work like 'red' and 'not-red'. Supposing all other things to be equal, the fact that an object is powerful rather than not-powerful does not seem to be a reason for preserving it over an object that is not-powerful. Of course, this is not to say that it might not be better (in some sense) if there existed an intelligent, benevolent, just, etc., person who is powerful rather than an intelligent, benevolent, just, etc., person who is not-powerful. Greater good would probably result in the first case than in the second. The first situation would be a better *situation* than the second. But this does not show that a being who is an intelligent, benevolent, just, etc., person would be a better *being* (or even a better person) if it were powerful rather than not-powerful. It would be better for the people of Utah if a man who is intelligent, benevolent, just, etc., were made governor of Utah rather than being allowed to function in a capacity in which he has no in-

The Justification of the Doctrine of Timelessnes: Anselm

fluence on public policy. But this does not show that the man who is intelligent, benevolent, just, etc., would be a better individual if he were made governor of Utah than he would be if he were allowed to function in a non-influential position.

I think this same set of remarks holds for a rather wide range of the other attributes traditionally assigned to God. Try 'immutable' on the first door and 'not-immutable' on the second. If the only thing we know about an object is that it cannot change, I cannot see that this would give us reason for preserving it over an object that can change. If might be better if there existed an intelligent, benevolent, wise, etc., being that cannot change rather than a similar being that can change. We could then be assured that the being in question would not cease to be intelligent, benevolent, wise, etc. But this does not show that the inability to change is, itself, a value-making feature of objects. Considering just the objects in question, the intelligent, benevolent, wise, etc., being that can change would appear to be as valuable as the intelligent, benevolent, wise, etc., being that cannot change. It is not until the first being *does* change (losing intelligence, wisdom, etc.) that a difference in value is detectable. I'm inclined to think that we get the same result when we write 'simple' (having no parts) and 'independent' on the first door and their contradictories on the second. I can't see that there would be any right choice between alternatives in these cases given the rules of the game we are playing. No one of these concepts seems to be connected with the notion of an object that ought to be preserved.

Try 'useful' on the first door and 'not-useful' on the second. In turn, write 'mother's favourite' and 'sweet-smelling' on the first door and their contradictories on the second. If an object is useful, that would be a reason for preserving it. If an object is mother's favourite or sweet-smelling, that would also be a reason for preserving it. The contradictories of these qualities do not name value-making features of things. On the two assumptions employed above (*viz.*, (1) that all value-making features of objects can characterize the same object, and (2) that an object is more or less valuable depending on how closely its value-making features approximate their exemplary versions), it will follow that if God is a being a more worthy of preservation than which cannot be conceived, God will possess the exemplary-version of, for example, sweet-smellingness.

(c) I have now finished with the practice interpretation of 'greater' in the formula: 'God is a being greater than which cannot be conceived.' Before leaving this preliminary discussion, however perhaps I should make clear why I have delayed us as long as I have with this practice session.

In the first place, the practice game has permitted us to make clear a procedure by which to argue that a given quality term (e.g., 'conscious' or 'omniscient') is attached logically to the notion of a being a greater than which cannot be conceived. This procedure will be indispensable in the discussion to follow. The warm-up has been, in part, a tool-building session. But secondly, and even more importantly, in the course of our deliberation, the practice interpretation of 'greater' has been shown to be inadequate. This is of interest in that it brings into focus what would be required of an *adequate* interpretation of this value-concept. Let me elaborate this point.

According to Anselm, the statement 'God is a being a greater than which cannot be conceived' is a way of formulating *our concept* of God. But our concept of God is the concept of a being that is omnipotent, immutable, perfectly good, perfectly just, and the like. It is not the concept of a being that is e.g., sweet-smelling. Thus, if on a given interpretation of 'greater', the statement 'God is a being a greater than which cannot be conceived' entails 'God is sweet-smelling', but does not entail 'God is omnipotent' or 'God is immutable', we know that on the interpretation in question Anselm's formula does not express *our* concept of God. A fully adequate interpretation of 'greater' would be one that renders Anselm's formula capable of entailing all of the divine attribution-statements usually endorsed within the Judeo-Christian religious tradition. It would also be such as not to entail statements that are blatantly and obviously not acceptable as characterizations of the Christian God, e.g., 'God is sweet-smelling'. An interpretation of 'greater' is more or less adequate depending on how well it fares when measured in accordance with these two principles of adequacy.

IV

In Pt. I, sec. 4 of *Anselm's Discovery*, Charles Hartshorne writes as follows:[6]

> But what is the meaning (of the term 'God')? Anselm replied with great simplicity: to be God is to be, such that 'none greater could be conceived'. And if you ask about the import of 'greater', the reply is, x is greater than y in so far as x is, and y is not, something 'which it is better to be than not to be'. Greater thus means superior, more excellent, more worthy of admiration and respect. Why does our Saint choose this definition? I suppose because he takes it for granted that by 'God' is meant the universal object of worship, and if God could have a superior, then only the ignorant or superstitious could worship Him – not all creatures, nor any reasonable creatures. They might fear or admire Him, but not rightly love Him in the unstained way which is worship.

I want now to examine the formula 'God is a being a greater than which cannot be conceived' using the interpretation of 'greater' that is suggested in this passage.

(*a*) In an article entitled 'On Using the Word "God"', H. N. Wieman characterizes the worship-reaction as involving feelings and attitudes '... such as awe, reverence, self-giving, supreme devotion, a sovereign love and loyalty as to what is felt to be most important not only for oneself but for all men who belong to the tribe'.[7] Wieman goes on to say that the term 'God' is correctly applied to anything that 'rightly engenders the worship-reaction', i.e., to anything that is an appropriate, fitting, worthy or rightful object of worship. If we could assume with St. Thomas that the term 'God' is a singular form of the class-term (count noun) 'god' – a term used when the speaker believes and means to be communicating the idea that there is one and only one member of this class[8] – we might then formulate Wieman's view as follows: Propositions of the form '*x* is god' mean '*x* is *an* appropriate, fitting, worthy or rightful object of worship'. Propositions of the form '*x* is God', mean '*x* is *the* (one and only) appropriate, fitting, worthy or rightful object of worship'. These analyses have been used by a number of contemporary philosophers of religion.[9] There are traces of them as well in some traditional theological sources.[10]

Now, on Hartshorne's account, the function '*x* is God' means '*x* is a being a greater than which cannot be conceived'. 'Greater' in this formula means 'superior, more excellent, more worthy of admiration and respect'. As Hartshorne moves along through the rest of his text, he seems constantly to be supposing that 'greater' means 'more worthy of worship'.[11] I think he intends is to be saying that the statement 'God is a being a greater than which cannot be conceived' means 'God is a being a more worthy of worship than which cannot be conceived'. Of course, if this is what Hartshorne is suggesting (and I shall assume for the rest of this discussion that this is so), Hartshorne's analysis of the function '*x* is God' cannot be strictly identified with the one proposed by Wieman. '*x* is the (one and only) object worthy of worship' is not equivalent to the function '*x* is a being a more worthy of worship than which cannot be conceived'. Suppose there existed just one being that is worthy of worship. This being would be the one and only object worthy of worship, but it might not be a being a more worthy of worship than which cannot be conceived. We might be able to *conceive* of a being that would be more worthy of worship than the one that is, in fact, the only being worthy of worship.[12]

(*b*) I now want to revise the two-door game.
There are two doors. On the first is written the name of a

quality and on the second is written the contradictory of the name written on the first. We are told that the qualities mentioned on the front of the doors characterize the objects behind them. We are also told that one of the objects is *worthy of worship*. The game is to choose the door concealing the object that is worthy of worship.

Let's begin by writing 'conscious' on the first door and 'not-conscious' on the second. As it was when playing the first version of the two-door game, the door marked 'conscious' would appear to be the right choice. Why? Hartshorne hints of a line of reasoning that might be used to justify this decision.[13] This line is developed in more detail by J. N. Findlay in 'Can God's Existence be Disproved?'[14] What I shall say in the next five paragraphs is intended as an interpretative-expansion of what I think is valuable (though not necessarily correct) in the remarks made by Hartshorne and Findlay on this topic.

The worshipper prays: 'Oh God, deliver me.' He acts as if he believes that the object of his worship is able to understand his plea. The worshipper sings praises and makes sacrifices. He acts as if he believes that the object of his worship will take notice of these actions. It would seem that to worship a given object (x) is to act as if one believes x to be conscious and aware. Let's entertain the following generalization: Any complex mode of behaviour that could not be described in a statement of the form 'A acts as if he believes x to be conscious or aware' could not be described as a genuine case of worship.

It should be noticed that the generalization I have just formulated does not imply that genuine worship is always directed toward an object that is, in fact, conscious and aware. What Hartshorne calls 'superstitious' and 'unreasonable' men might think that a given object is conscious when it is not. Such men might act as if they believe an object to be conscious even though the object is not of this sort. There is a second point too. The thesis we are examining does not require that a worshipper actually believe that the object of his worship is conscious. I can fear an object that is not dangerous or threatening. I can also fear an object that I do not really believe to be dangerous or threatening. The first case might involve nothing more than a mistaken belief on my part. The second case might be an instance of emotional maladjustment. If one suffers from a phobia, one might fear an object even though one is intellectually convinced that the object in question is not dangerous or threatening. Here we have a case of genuine fear although the object that is feared is not believed to be dangerous or threatening. I think we must allow at least the logical possibility of a parallel case with respect to worship. A man might worship an object though he does not actually believe that the object of worship is conscious or aware. This would be a pathological worship syndrome, but it might still have to count as a case of genuine worship. On the thesis formulated above, if we are dealing with a case of genuine worship, the worshipper behaves *as if* he believes that the object of worship is conscious or aware. This generalization allows for the case of genuine worship in which the worshipper does not actually believe that the object is conscious or aware.

How might one show that a given object is *not* a proper or appropriate object of worship? If the remarks just made about the logic of 'worship' could be accepted, I think one could show that a given object is not an appropriate object of worship if one could show that the object in question is not conscious or aware. The argument follows:

(1) To worship x is to act as if one believes x to be conscious or aware.

(2) If x is not conscious or aware, then to act toward x as if one believes x to be conscious or aware is to act in a way that is inappropriate and unfitting to x's nature.

(3) Therefore: If x is not conscious and aware, to worship x is to act toward x in a way that is inappropriate and unfitting to x's nature.

(4) If to worship x is to act in a way that is inappropriate and unfitting to x's nature, then x is not an appropriate or

The Justification of the Doctrine of Timelessness: Anselm

fitting object of worship. (This premise follows from the fact that if x is an appropriate or fitting object of worship, then to worship x is to act toward x in a way that is appropriate and fitting to x's nature.)

(5) Therefore: If x is not conscious and aware, x is not an appropriate object of worship. 'x is worthy of worship' *entails* 'x is conscious and aware'.

If an object is not dangerous or threatening, then although one might fear it, it would not be an appropriate or fitting object of fear. To be afraid of such an object would be unreasonable, unjustified, queer, or pathological. As Findlay points out, this conclusion is derived from an analysis of the notion of fear. This is to say (as I am understanding the matter), this conclusion is derived from an analysis of the behaviour patterns involved in standard cases of genuine fear. In the same way, on the proposal now before us, if an object is not conscious and aware, it is not an appropriate or fitting object of worship. Although one might worship such an object, one's worship-attitude would have to be counted as unreasonable, unjustified, queer, or pathological. This claim is (presumably) based on an analysis of the notion of worship, i.e., on an analysis of the behaviour patterns involved in standard cases of genuine worship.

The following extension of the reasoning just reviewed seems to me to warrant careful consideration: When the worshipper prays: 'Oh God, deliver me', he acts as if the object of his worship has power and knowledge enough to deliver him from his plight. Characteristically, the worshipper makes gestures of submission (bowing the head, bending the knee, prostrating the body, etc.) – gestures that express the belief that the worshipper is to some extent under the control (subject to the power) of the object toward which the worship behaviour is directed. These observations suggest the following generalization: Any complex mode of behaviour that could not be described in sentences of the form, 'A acts as if he believes x to be powerful and knowledgeable' could not be counted as cases of genuine worship.

If this is right (and I'm not really sure that it is), an argument of the form just employed with respect to the property of being conscious might be used to show that the function '*x* is worthy of worship, *entails* '*x* is powerful' and '*x* is knowledgeable'.

Move now to Anselm's formula. We are reading it as follows: 'God is a being a more worthy of worship than which cannot be conceived.' By the reasoning set out above, we establish that the property of being conscious is a value-making (call it a 'holy-making') feature of objects. If we then assumed that it is logically possible for all holy-making features to attach to one object (Leibniz's principle), the results of our first turn with the revised two-door game would allow us to conclude that Anselm's formula entails 'God is conscious'. If an argument of the form used to justify the selection of the door marked 'conscious' could be used to justify the selection of the door marked 'powerful' and 'knowledgeable', we could also conclude that Anselm's formula, as presently interpreted, entails 'God is powerful' and 'God is knowledgeable'. Given a second assumption, *viz.*, that a being is more or less worthy of worship depending on how closely its holy-making features approach their exemplary versions, we could conclude, further, that Anselm's formula entails 'God is omnipotent' and 'God is omniscient' – where 'omnipotent' and 'omniscient' name the exemplary versions of the properties named by 'powerful' and 'knowledgeable' respectively. If a being were anything less than omnipotent or omniscient, we could at least conceive of a being more worthy of worship than it, *viz.*, one just like it except for being omnipotent and omniscient.

We are now ready to make what seems to me to be a rather interesting observation.

Write 'benevolent' on the first door and 'not-benevolent' on the second door. I'm sure that Hartshorne and Findlay (as well as Anselm) would insist that the right choice in this case would be the door marked 'benevolent'. However, it seems to me that an argument of the sort just used to

The Justification of the Doctrine of Timelessnes: Anselm

justify the choice of the door marked 'conscious' ('powerful', 'knowledgeable') could not be successfully employed to justify the choice of the door marked 'benevolent'. Let me expand this point.

Consider the following generalization: To worship an object (x) is to act as if one believes x to be benevolent. Any complex mode of behaviour not desirable in sentences of the form, 'A acts as if he believes x to be benevolent' could not be counted as a case of genuine worship. Given the truth of this comment about the logic of 'worship', the rest of the argument-pattern used above could then be employed to show that the function 'x is worthy of worship' *entails* 'x is benevolent'. But the trouble with this line of reasoning is that the initial generalization upon which the argument rests is openly and obviously false. If it were true, devil worship (Black Mass) could not be regarded as genuine worship. When one worships the devil one does not behave as if one believes the object of his worship is benevolent (quite the reverse). But devil worship is genuine worship. To judge otherwise would be absurd – it would be to preserve the term 'worship' for one's own special purposes. Surely, the initial generalization we are now considering cannot be taken as an adequate comment on the logic of 'worship'.

At this point I could imagine someone arguing as follows: Although devil worship is genuine worship, it is immoral in that it is sacrilegious. But if one *ought not* to worship an object lacking the property of benevolence, such an object should not be counted as *worthy* of worship. An object that is worthy of worship is such that it *ought to be* worshipped.

This argument rests on a confusion.[15] If I were to propose marriage to the *Mona Lisa*, I would be acting inappropriately with respect to this object. The *Mona Lisa* is not (what might be called) a *logically* appropriate object of the emotions and appetites expressed by this action. The action would reveal that I had made a factual mistake about the features of the *Mona Lisa* or that I was suffering from a pathological condition akin to phobia. But now let's suppose that I propose marriage to Mrs. Jones who is happily married to Mr. Jones. Here, my action would not be logically inappropriate, though it might be morally or socially improper. Mrs. Jones would be a logically appropriate, though not a morally appropriate object of my romantic affections. Now, on Findlay's understanding of the matter, the terms 'worthy', 'fitting', 'appropriate', etc., occurring in the function 'x is a worthy, appropriate, fitting, etc., object of worship' do the same job of work as is done by the same terms occurring in the function 'x is a worthy, appropriate, fitting, etc., object of fear'. Further, on Findlay's account, we uncover the properties a thing must have in order to count as a worthy, appropriate or fitting object of fear by an analysis of the meaning of the term 'fear'. This is to say that we discover these properties by examining the behaviour patterns associated with standard cases of genuine fear. It is clear, I think, that 'worthy' carries no moral connotations in this context. We are here trying to uncover the properties a thing must have in order to count as a *logically* appropriate object of fear or worship. The *moral* status of a given case of fear or worship is not at issue in this discussion. I could imagine someone holding that in no case is fear, romantic attachment or worship morally improper. He might still insist on a list of properties which are such that if an object lacked them, it would not qualify as a logically appropriate object of fear, romantic feelings or worship. In this sense, then, 'x is worthy of worship' does not entail 'x is benevolent'. There are at least some cases of genuine worship (whatever their moral status may be) that cannot be described in sentences of the form, 'A acts as if he believes x to be benevolent'.

It seems to me that in the present game, if Hartshorne, Findlay, and Anselm are to justify the choice of the door marked 'benevolent', the argument they must use is as follows: The object that is worthy of worship might be behind the door marked 'benevolent'. It might also be behind the door marked 'not-benevolent'. Both are possi-

The Justification of the Doctrine of Timelessness: Anselm

bilities. But if an object is benevolent, that is a *reason* for worshipping it. 'I worship *x* because *x* is benevolent' might not be conclusive, but it is sensible. However, if a thing is not benevolent (so the argument goes), that would not be a reason for worshipping it. 'I worship *x* because *x* is not benevolent' is not sensible. If a non-benevolent object is an appropriate object of worship (e.g., the devil) it is so because it has features *other* than non-benevolence (e.g., consciousness, power, knowledge, etc.) that account for this fact.

This argument has the structure of the arguments used with respect to all of the properties treated in the *first* version of the two-door game – the one making use of the value-concept defined in terms of the ethical notion 'ought to be preserved'. When following out the details of that game we did not argue that specific qualities were *entailed* by the function '*x* is worthy of preservation'. We argued only that if a thing is, e.g., conscious, that is a *reason* for preserving it while if a thing is not conscious, that is not a reason for preserving it. What I am now suggesting is that if the door marked 'benevolent' is to be chosen in the second version of the two-door game, this choice can be justified (if at all) only by way of the pattern of argument utilized when working with the first version of the game. (This was one of the reasons for working as long as we did with the first version of the game.)

Let's move again to Anselm's formula. God is a being a more worthy of preservation than which cannot be conceived. By the reasoning just reviewed, we establish that benevolence is a holy-making feature of objects. Given the two assumptions introduced above – *viz.*, it is logically possible for a single being to possess all holy-making features of objects (Leibniz's principle); and, an object is more or less worthy of worship depending on how closely its holy-making features approach to their exemplary versions – we can conclude that an object a more worthy of worship than which cannot be conceived would have to possess the exemplary version of benevolence, i.e., *perfect* benevolence. 'God is a being a more worthy of worship than that which

God and Timelessness

cannot be conceived' *entails* 'God is perfectly benevolent'.

In the second chapter of the *Idea of the Holy*, Rudolf Otto claimed that as originally understood, the concept of the holy included only the conceptual ingredients described in his book under the heading of the *Mysterium Tremendum*. On Otto's account, the notion of the *Mysterium Tremendum* includes the ideas of power and knowledge, but it does not include the moral meaning-elements designated by such predicates as 'benevolent', 'just', 'merciful', etc. According to Otto, these last mentioned items were later additions to the concept of the holy. The original concept did not require that the holy be a *moral* being.

I want neither to endorse nor to reject Otto's historical thesis. What I should like to point out, however, is that there may be a *logical* distinction within the concept of the holy that corresponds more or less closely to the historical distinction made by Otto. Given the line of thinking examined above, '*x* is worthy of worship' *entails* some of the predicates usually used to characterize the Christian God (e.g., 'conscious' and, perhaps, 'powerful' and 'knowledgeable'), but it does not entail others. Moral predicates such as 'benevolent' seem to fall into this second category. Of course, this is not to say that predicates such as 'benevolent' bear *no* logical connection to the function '*x* is worthy of worship'. If (as suggested above) the possession of benevolence counts as a *reason* for worshipping an object, then it must be listed among the holy-making features of things. A logical connection of this latter sort, however, is considerably weaker than entailment.

Let us suppose that the logical distinction just suggested is sound. It is interesting to notice that it could not have been made had we been working exclusively with Anselm's formula. On the view examined above, the function '*x* is a being a greater than which cannot be conceived' bears an *entailment* relation to '*x* is perfectly benevolent' as well as to '*x* is conscious'. This is so even if the properties mentioned in these two latter statement-forms bear different logical relations to the idea expressed in the *diminished* function '*x* is

The Justification of the Doctrine of Timelessnes: Anselm

worthy of worship'. Anselm's formula has a whirlwind effect in this matrix of related ideas. Given the adequacy of the reasoning sketched above, Anselm's statement indifferently entails a whole range of predication-statements that have very different logical connections to the route idea of the holy.

This last point suggests another. According to Hartshorne, the statement, 'God is a being a more worthy of worship than which cannot be conceived' is to be understood as the *definition* of the term 'God'. If this statement entails 'God is conscious', 'God is omnipotent', 'God is perfectly benevolent', and the like, these latter must then be regarded as *analytic* statements. Still, if the reasoning set forth above could be accepted, we should have to recognize a difference in the way the various qualities mentioned in these analytic predication-statements relate to the route idea of the holy, i.e., to the idea expressed in the function '*x* is worthy of worship'. Even if one held that all of the traditional divine attribute-terms attach analytically to the title-term 'God', one could still make out a sense in which some of God's attributes are more *fundamental* than others. This would be an interesting finding. Offhand, one would think it impossible to make a distinction of this sort among the properties mentioned in *analytic* predication-statements. As regards bachelors, I doubt if one could decide whether being a man or being unmarried is more fundamental to the concept.

(*c*) Hartshorne says that 'greater' in the statement 'God is a being a greater than which cannot be conceived' means 'more worthy of worship'. He thus proposes that Anselm's formula be understood as meaning 'God is a being a more worthy of worship than which cannot be conceived'. Making use of two assumptions (*viz.*, it is logically possible that all holy-making features of objects attach to the same being; and, an object is more or less worthy of worship depending on how closely its holy-making features approach to their exemplary versions), I have tried to identify two ways in which one might argue that a statement assigning a specific attribute to God might be justified by reference to this statement. One might argue that the diminished formula 'x is worthy of worship' *entails* 'x is ϕ' (e.g., 'x is powerful') and thus that 'x is a being a greater than which cannot be conceived' entails 'x is perfectly ϕ' (e.g., 'x is omnipotent'). On the other hand, one might argue that although 'x is ϕ' (e.g., 'x is benevolent') is not entailed by 'x is worthy of worship', the possession of ϕ constitutes a reason for worshipping x whereas the possession of not-ϕ does not constitute a reason for worshipping x. In this latter case, although 'x is ϕ' is not entailed by 'x is worthy of worship', ϕ still counts as a holy-making feature of things and thus 'x is a being a more worthy of worship than which cannot be conceived' still entails 'x is perfectly ϕ' (e.g., 'x is perfectly benevolent').

Do we now have a workable method for justifying propositions assigning specific qualities to God? I'm not really sure. There are difficulties buried in the above discussion that I am aware of but have not identified in the interest of brevity and clarity. There are probably other difficulties that I have not thought of at all. Still, I know of no more promising interpretation of Anselm's formula than the one proposed by Hartshorne; and I know of no better way of understanding Anselm's procedure for justifying divine predication-statements than the one I have outlined above. If this is not a correct interpretation of Anselm's statement; and if this is not an adequate justification-procedure for statements assigning attributes to God, the conclusion might be that Anselm's thinking about the concept of God is incapable of precise clarification and that Anselm's whole approach to the problem of justifying doctrines about the nature of God is deficient – perhaps even basically misguided.

V

Having spent considerable time trying to clarify the procedure by which Anselm attempts to justify statements

The Justification of the Doctrine of Timelessness: Anselm

attributing specific attributes to God, we come now to the issue of central concern in this chapter. The question is: Does the statement, 'God is a being a greater than which cannot be conceived', entail the statement, 'God is timeless'?

Assume for the moment that 'greater' in the phrase 'greater than which cannot be conceived' is to be understood as Hartshorne suggests. How could one argue that the statement 'God is a being a greater than which cannot be conceived' entails 'God is timeless'?

Referring back to the two argument-patterns summarized at the end of the last section, we might try an argument of the first sort, i.e., one having the structure of the argument examined when working with the predicate 'conscious'. This would require that we begin with the claim that to worship an object is (in part) to behave toward that object as if one believed it to be timeless. No doubt, verbal behaviour would be the only relevant behaviour to consider. But, surely, this generalization would be mistaken. Pagans worship trees and mountains. Though this may be unreasonable or even pathological, it is surely genuine worship; and it does not involve behaviour describable as: 'A acts as if he believes x to be timeless'. Thus, it would appear that if we are to argue that 'God is timeless' is entailed by 'God is a being a greater than which cannot be conceived', we would have to seek a form of argument other than this. The second form of argument outlined above (i.e., the one examined when dealing with the predicate 'benevolent') would appear to be the one we should use. So much seems to me to be apparent.

Hartshorne and Wieman maintain (and I think rightly) that the worship attitude involves feelings of awe, respect, admiration, devotion, love, loyalty, and the like. Would the fact that a thing is timeless be a *relevant* thing to mention when attempting to justify these feelings or attitudes toward it? At what point would the fact that a thing is timeless connect with this cluster of emotions?

According to Rudolf Otto, if one is awe-struck, one is disposed to 'tremble' and 'shudder'. Awe is the reaction one has when confronted with that which is 'overpowering' and which is also weird, eerie and uncanny. It is the feeling expressed in such phrases as, 'it makes my blood run cold', 'it makes my flesh creep'. It is an emotion akin to fear and dread.[16] If this is right (or nearly right), I can see no clear connection between timelessness and the emotion of awe. If a thing is timeless this does not suggest that it is overpowering — quite the reverse (Ch. 6). If a thing is timeless, this doesn't seem to bear on the question of whether it is eerie or weird either. The number two is timeless, but I can find no reason to think that it is uncanny. The number two has no effect on me that I could describe in the phrase 'it makes my blood run cold' or 'it makes my flesh creep'.

Respect and loyalty are attitudes that are appropriately directed toward a given individual when that individual is related to one in a certain way (one's king or one's mother) or when that individual performs actions that exhibit strength, courage, care, concern, etc. If a timeless individual were related to me in the requisite ways, or if a timeless individual were to perform actions that exhibit strength, courage, care, concern, etc., it might then count as an appropriate object of my respect and loyalty. However, if a timeless being were to count as an appropriate object of my respect or loyalty, I think that this would be due to the fact that it is related to me in the requisite way or performs actions of the sort just described. I do not think that it could be an appropriate object of my respect or loyalty *because* it is timeless. It would be strange to have feelings of respect or loyalty for the number two. And the fact that the number two is timeless does nothing to mitigate this strangeness. I think that remarks similar to this hold as well for the attitude of love — at least the kind of love that involves feelings of respect and loyalty.

Putting aside questions about respect and loyalty, I think that one might *admire* a timeless being in the way in which one admires a beautiful painting or a majestic mountain. I think, too, that one might admire a timeless being in this way just because it is timeless. In *this* sense, I think one might *love* a timeless being and cite its lack of temporal position

The Justification of the Doctrine of Timelessness: Anselm

and temporal extension as the reason for one's love. But after this much is acknowledged, there seems to me to be a subtle and difficult question remaining, *viz.*, whether the fact that a given individual is timeless could be cited in support of the claim that the individual in question is a *fitting* or *appropriate* object of admiration, i.e., whether the fact that a thing is timeless would count as a reason for thinking that the thing in question is admir*able*. A man might admire his wife because she is bald. 'How majestic to be bald – how dignified and beautiful her baldness makes her.' We would probably hesitate to say that this judgement is unreasonable, or pathological. More so than when dealing with fear, respect or loyalty, we leave a lot of room for *taste* as regards admiration. It is probably true that a number of important religious thinkers have admired what is timeless precisely because it is timeless. But it is not at all clear to me that the lack of temporal position and temporal extension has a bearing on the question of whether a thing is admir*able*. I say again, the issue before us is difficult and confusing. When I say that it is not clear to me that the possession of timelessness has a bearing on whether a given object is admirable, I do not mean to say that it *is* clear to me that it does *not* have such a bearing. I'm simply stopped on this question. I can find no grounds for judgement one way or the other.

Let's try the following response to our original problem. We know that if an object is more worthy of worship than which cannot be conceived, that object is, e.g., powerful, benevolent, knowledgeable, etc. We know, too, that if an object is timeless, it is immutable in the strong sense of 'immutable' (Ch. 3). But, so the argument continues, it would be better if an object that is powerful and benevolent were such that it could not change than it would be if that object were such that it could change. We could then be assured that the object in question would not cease to be powerful and benevolent. However, this kind of argument will not show that timelessness (or, for that matter, immutability) is a holy-making feature of objects. At very best this sort of argument could show only that the situation in which a powerful and benevolent being is timeless is a better *situation* than one in which a powerful and benevolent being is not timeless. It might be better (for us, or in general) if a powerful and benevolent being were timeless rather than temporal, but this would not show that the individual in question would be a better *individual* if he were timeless rather than temporal. (We encountered this sort of problem when dealing with omnipotence and immutability in the first version of the two-door game.)

These last reflections suggest yet another way in which one might attempt to argue that timelessness is a holy-making feature of objects. Let us assume that a being more worthy of worship than which cannot be conceived would have to be immutable in the strong sense of 'immutable' formulated in Ch. 3. Perhaps an immutable being would be more awful or more worthy of respect or devotion than a mutable being. In Ch. 3 I argued that 'x is timeless' entails 'x is immutable' – in the strong sense of 'immutable'. I also sketched an argument designed to show that if an individual is immutable in the strong sense of 'immutable', that individual would have to be timeless. If this second argument could be accepted, we could now conclude that a being a more worthy of worship than which cannot be conceived would have to be timeless. 'x is timeless' is entailed by 'x is immutable' (in the strong sense); and 'immutable' (in the strong sense) names a holy-making feature of objects.

In the next chapter I shall register some misgivings about the claim that the sense of 'immutable' involved in this argument (what I have called the strong sense of 'immutable', i.e., the *logical* incapability of change) is connected logically to the notion of a being that is worthy of worship. But quite apart from any difficulties that might arise with respect to this part of the argument we are now considering, there seems to me to be an important problem connected with the idea that 'x is timeless' is entailed by 'x is immutable' (in the strong sense). In Ch. 3, I rejected St. Thomas's effort to establish this thesis. I then did the best I could to support it with an argument of my own. But, as was noted at the very end of Ch. 3, the argument I proposed in place of the one offered by St. Thomas is not conclusive. It involves a number of assumptions that are far from obvious. Thus, it seems to me that there is a lot of work yet to be done by one who would support the doctrine of timelessness in the way now under examination. One thing that is very badly needed is a really convincing display of the logical support underpinning the claim that 'x is immutable' (in the strong sense) entails 'x is timeless'.

I have two concluding remarks to make on this general topic: (1) It may be that the statement 'God is a being a greater than which cannot be conceived' means 'God is a being a more worthy of worship than which cannot be conceived' and that I am not seeing the connection between the general formula and the statement 'God is timeless'. If this is true, then I must ask those who would justify the doctrine of God's timelessness by reference to Anselm's formula to make this connection clear to me. (2) It may be that the statement, 'God is a being a greater than which cannot be conceived' does not mean 'God is a being more worthy of worship than which cannot be conceived', and that when the proper interpretation of this general formula is finally uncovered, it will be found to entail 'God is timeless'. In this case, I must ask those who hold this view to provide the interpretation in question. I have exhausted my resources on this question. Though I have tried to look at the matter sympathetically, I have been unable to discover any clear logical connection between the idea that God is a being a greater than which cannot be conceived and the idea that God is timeless.

NOTES

[1] *The Ontological Argument*, edited by A. Plantinga, New York, Doubleday, 1965, pp. 141-2.

[2] *Monologium*, Ch. XV. This passage translated by D. Dean, St. Anselm, La Salle, Open Court, 1958, pp. 62-3.

God and Timelessness

[3] *Monologium*, Ch. XV, Dean translation, pp. 62–3.
[4] *The Ontological Argument*, edited by A. Plantinga, p. 143.
[5] *Monologium*, Ch. XV, Dean translation, p. 63.
[6] La Salle, Open Court, 1965; pp. 25–6.
[7] *Journal of Philosophy*, Vol. 30 (1933), pp. 401–2.
[8] *Summa Theologica*, Pt. I. Q. 13, A. 9.
[9] See, for example, J. N. Findlay's 'Can God's Existence be Disproved?', reprinted in *The Ontological Argument*, ed. A. Plantinga, sec. I; H. D. Aiken's 'God and Evil: A Study of Some Relations Between Faith and Morals', *Ethics*, v. 68 (1958); and E. S. Brightman's *The Problem of God*, New York, Abington Press, 1930, esp. Ch. V.
[10] In his *Reply to Faustus the Manichean*, St. Augustine says that the object worshipped by the Manicheans is not *a god* because even if it did exist (which it does not) it would not be a 'proper object of worship' (Bk. XX, numbered paragraphs 5 and 9). He adds that the object worshipped by Christians is the only *true God* because it alone is the object to which worship (*Latria*) is due (Bk. XXI, numbered paragraphs 17–21).
[11] See, for example, pp. 29, 40 and 113 of *Anselm's Discovery*.
[12] In the *Problem of God* (Ch. V), E. S. Brightman says that the function 'x is God' means 'x is worthy of worship'. He also holds that God exists and is limited in both knowledge and power. He thus agrees that although there exists one and only one being that is worthy of worship, that being is not a being more worthy of worship than which cannot be conceived. It would be an even more appropriate object of worship if it were unlimited as regards its knowledge and power.
[13] I refer here to secs. 4 and 5 where Hartshorne seems to derive the claim that God is unsurpassable from an analysis of what it is to engage in an act of worship.
[14] See especially pp. 114–15 of *The Ontological Argument*, ed. A. Plantinga.
[15] I am indebted to Robert Adams of the University of Michigan for clarifying the distinction made in this paragraph. The example following is his.
[16] *The Idea of the Holy*; translated by J. W. Harvey; New York, Oxford University Press, 1958; Ch. IV.

9
The Justification of the Doctrine of Timelessness: Schleiermacher

I

According to Schleiermacher, religion has its centre in a certain feeling, consciousness or awareness. In *The Christian Faith*, this consciousness is characterized as the 'feeling of absolute dependence'.[1] Further, Schleiermacher says that the occurrence of this feeling in a given individual invariably results in the need to give it expression. Such expression may take the form of bodily gestures (e.g., worship gestures) and it almost always takes shape in some kind of verbal expression. On the most immediate level, verbal expression is usually cast in poetical or figurative form. After some development it is formulated in propositions.[2] When a given religious proposition articulates the content of the religious awareness of a number of individuals and is thus endorsed by those individuals as formulating what they know to be true on the basis of direct awareness, the proposition in question acquires the status of a religious 'dogma' ('*Glaubenssatz*'). To say of a religious proposition that it is a dogma is to say that it formulates a religious belief held in common by the members of a given religious community. A dogma is always a dogma relative to some particular religious community, e.g., a Christian dogma, a Protestant dogma, a Catholic dogma, etc.[3]

What now of the enterprise of dogmatic theology? The

dogmatic theologian is charged with the task of formulating, clarifying and systematizing dogma. He is that member of a given religious community who undertakes to explicate and organize the set of religious propositions endorsed within the community of which he is a member.[4] On this account, there is no such thing as a theologian *per se*. A theologian is a theologian relative to a certain religious community. There are, e.g., Protestant theologians, Catholic theologians and, perhaps, just Christian theologians – depending on the community for which they intend to be speaking, i.e., depending on the specific set of religious dogmas they are attempting to explicate and organize.

How then are we to judge a given theological proposal? Schleiermacher insists on two broad measures of adequacy.

First, a given dogmatic proposal has what Schleiermacher calls 'scientific value' in so far as (1) it is clear and definite as regards its propositional content; (2) it is internally consistent and logically coherent with other dogmas of the religious community for which the theologian is speaking; and (3) it is 'fruitful', i.e., it 'opens up', 'points towards', and in general *enlightens* other dogmas held in the community.[5] Dogmatics, like any other undertaking aimed at the construction of a system of propositions, is subject to the normal standards of clarity, logical consistency and conceptual coherence.

Secondly, Schleiermacher says that a given theological proposal has 'ecclesiastical value' in so far as it succeeds in articulating the belief 'norm' of the relevant religious community. Since this belief 'norm' is, itself, determined by the specific nature of the religious consciousness of the individuals making up the community, ultimately the 'ecclesiastical value' of a given theological proposal is a function of the adequacy with which it formulates an 'element' of the religious feeling shared by the members of the religious community for which the theologian speaks.[6] No matter how clear and consistent a given dogmatic proposal may be, it may fail to formulate the *content* of a belief held in the religious community. When this happens, the proposal is,

The Justification of the Doctrine of Timelessness: Schleiermacher

in a sense, 'materially inadequate'. It cannot be taken as the formulation of a dogma, regardless of how well it qualifies on the various 'scientific' criteria mentioned above.

Let's see if we can get a little clearer about this second test of adequacy.

How shall we decide whether a given theological proposal succeeds in articulating part of the belief 'norm' of a given religious community? This is to ask: How shall we decide whether a given proposal formulates some 'element' of the religious feeling shared by the members of a church? I have been unable to find a passage in which Schleiermacher addresses himself to this question in its general form, but if we restrict attention to Christian theology, and more particularly, to Evangelical (Protestant) theology, I think that Schleiermacher's view can be summarized as follows.

New Testament scripture contains a record of a large number of dogmatic propositions that are endorsed by the Christian community generally. Thus, in so far as a given theological proposal can be supported by reference to this source (reading the text sympathetically and drawing on broad themes rather than isolated statements) to that extent it is shown to be 'ecclesiastically' adequate. Of course, the reverse holds as well. In so far as a given theological proposal is at odds with the content of scripture, to that extent it is to be regarded as an 'ecclesiastically' inadequate formulation of Christian dogma. Moving now to the Evangelical sub-community of the Christian Church, the creeds and other confessional documents of the Evangelical Church contain the record of a number of propositions that articulate the belief 'norm' of this sub-community. Thus, a theological proposal that can be supported by reference to Evangelical confessional literature is to be regarded as an 'ecclesiastically' adequate formulation of Evangelical dogma. Of course, as above, the reverse holds as well. Schleiermacher adds that an appeal to the confessional literature is really an indirect appeal to Scripture. Nothing is contained in the creeds and confessions that is not, itself, documented by reference to Scripture. However, the confessional documents of the Evangelical Church bring out the distinctively 'Protestant content' of Scripture. For this reason, Schleiermacher says, the Protestant theologian is usually better advised to appeal to the confessional literature rather than to the immediate content of Scripture itself.[7]

What shall we do with a theological proposal that can neither be verified nor confuted by reference to Scripture or by reference to the confessional documents of the Evangelical Church? Schleiermacher says very little about this kind of case, but he suggests in one passage that the theologian might here make a direct appeal to the beliefs of the individuals making up the religious community. In this case, the theologian is appealing to that part of the belief 'norm' of the Church that has not been crystallized in Scripture or Creed.[8] Though there is a vague suggestion that reference to the writings of Christian teachers (e.g., the Church Fathers)[9] might be relevant here, Schleiermacher does not really clarify the form an effective appeal of this latter sort would take.

In the introduction to his textbook of scholastic theology, Father Joseph Pohle characterizes theology (in general) as follows:[10]

> Like all sciences, theology deduces unknown truths from known and certain principles, by means of correct conclusions. As a principle to reason from in his quest of truth the dogmatician receives, and believingly embraces the infallible truths of revelation, and by means of logical constructions, systematic groupings and correct deductions, erects upon this foundation a logical body of doctrine, as does the historian who works with the facts of history, or the jurist who deals with statutes, or the scientists who employ bodies and their phenomena as materials for scientific construction.

With respect to *dogmatics*, considered as a special branch of theology, Father Pohle continues as follows:[11]

> We define special dogmatics or dogmatic theology proper, after the example of Scheeben, as 'The scientific exposition of the entire domain of theoretical knowledge, which can be obtained from

The Justification of the Doctrine of Timelessness: Schleiermacher

divine Revelation, of God Himself and His Activity, based upon the dogmas of the Church ... A dogma is a norm of knowledge ... [which is] ultimately rooted in ... divine Revelation as contained in Holy Scripture and Tradition, and expounded by the Church.'

As a final comment, Father Pohle characterizes the special type of dogmatic theology known as 'Scholastic Dogmatic Theology' in the following way:[12]

Dogmatic Theology is called *Scholastic*, when assuming and utilizing the results of the positive method, it undertakes: (*a*) to unfold the deeper content of dogma; (*b*) to set forth the relations of different dogmas to one another; (*c*) by syllogistic process to deduce from given or certain premises so-called 'theological conclusions'; and (*d*) to make plausible, though, of course not to explain fully, to our weak human reason by means of philosophical meditation, and especially of proofs from analogy, the dogmas and mysteries of the Faith.

I think it is clear that Father Pohle is here agreeing – at least in general outline – with the characterization of dogmatic theology given by Schleiermacher. In particular, I think Pohle endorses the idea that a given dogmatic proposal must be judged in accordance with two quite distinct criteria. Dogmatics is a systematic science. The theologian aims for a clear and consistent body of doctrine. Dogmatics in thus subject to what Schleiermacher has labelled the 'scientific' tests of adequacy. But theology is not pure speculation. Like any science, Pohle says, dogmatics is subject to a kind of material criterion. He says that in this respect, it is like history or physics. The material with which the theologian works is 'Revelation'. The 'Revelation' consists of knowledge given in Scripture, tradition and the dogmatic pronouncements of the Church. At least in part, a given theological proposal must be judged by reference to how well it articulates the 'deeper content' of this knowledge. This seems to be precisely what Schleiermacher is saying when he insists that theological propositions are subject to an 'ecclesiastical' test of adequacy.

Let me risk a general formulation of what I take Schleiermacher and Pohle to be saying on this topic: The theologian

God and Timelessness

is charged with the task of clarifying and organizing dogma. Dogma is not something that the theologian makes up on his own. There is what might be called a 'datum discourse' of theology. This discourse consists primarily of Scripture, but it must be conceived of broadly enough to include such things as the traditional creeds, the other confessional documents of the religious community, the official dogmatic pronouncements of the Church and the beliefs of ordinary Christians through the generations. These items may be weighted differently by theologians representing different religious communities, e.g., Catholics will probably weigh the official pronouncements of the Church more heavily than will Protestants. The job of the dogmatic theologian is to formulate, clarify and organize the content of this datum discourse. In so far as the job is to formulate, clarify and organize, theology is subject to the various 'scientific' tests of adequacy. In so far as the job is to formulate, clarify and organize the *content of the datum discourse*, theology is subject to an 'ecclesiastical' criterion. The history of heresy is the history of theological attempts that have failed to pass this second test of adequacy.

II

A dogmatic proposal is 'scientifically' adequate in so far as it is clear and consistent; and in so far as it coheres logically and 'points toward' other dogmas constituting the 'norm' of the Faith. I want now to identify five general areas of concern regarding the 'scientific' adequacy of the claim that God is timeless.

(*a*) It could hardly escape notice that the doctrine of God's timelessness does not square well with the standard Christian belief that God once assumed finite, human form (the doctrine of the incarnation). As a man, of course, God had both temporal extension and temporal location. What would it be for a timeless being to *become* temporal? Was He timeless *before* He was temporal – say, in the year 1 B.C.?

The Justification of the Doctrine of Timelessness: Schleiermacher

But, of course, it is generally acknowledged by Christian theologians that the God-man paradox *is* a paradox. The claim that God assumed finite and temporal form is not *supposed* to fit well with other things that Christians believe about the nature of God. Perhaps this is a satisfactory reply. I shall not try to pursue this matter any further.

(*b*) Schleiermacher seems to have been aware of a logical tension between the idea that God is timeless and the standard interpretation of the Christian doctrine of divine creation. Schleiermacher also seems to have been alert to the internal friction involved in the claim that a timeless being is omnipotent. It is not at all obvious that a timeless individual can be consistently characterized as having *any* creative power let alone creative power that is unlimited or 'infinite'. We must add that there appears to be no obvious way of understanding the idea that a being existing 'outside of time' sustains or preserves the temporally extended universe of objects. (All of this was discussed at length in Ch. 6.)

These conflicts are of first importance. In his article on the topic of 'omnipotence' in the *Catholic Encyclopedia*,[18] J. A. McHugh says that God's omnipotence is to be understood as the ability to bring about or effect objects and states of affairs. He then says:

> The omnipotence of God is a dogma of the Catholic Faith, contained in all creeds and defined by various councils. In the Old Testament, there are more than seventy passages in which God is called *Shaddai*, i.e., omnipotent. The Scriptures represent this attribute as indefinite power which God alone has. The Greek and Latin Fathers unanimously teach the Doctrine of Divine Omnipotence.

I shall not quote the equally emphatic entries contained in this source concerning the dogmas of divine creation and divine preservation. The datum discourse of theology is clear and explicit on all three of these topics. There is no major (or minor) creed or catechism of either the Catholic or Protestant traditions that fails to mention the fact that God is the omnipotent Creator and Sustainer of the Universe. These are among the first things learned as a Christian. No synopsis of the Bible (Old or New Testaments) could fail to mention these theses. If the doctrine of timelessness conflicts with these three dogmas (or any one of these three dogmas) this must surely be taken as an important negative factor when estimating its 'scientific' value.

(*c*) Boethius introduced the notion of God's timelessness as a way of solving (or dissolving) the problem of divine foreknowledge (Ch. 4, sec. III, subsection *a*). If in fact, this doctrine does solve this problem (as seems to me to be likely) then this should be listed in its favour when estimating its 'scientific' value. However, I think there are at least two considerations that should cause some hesitations in this connection. In the first place, as we saw in Ch. 4, sec. III, subsection *b*, there is at least one other way in which the problem of divine foreknowledge might be handled. The line of thinking implicit in St. Augustine's treatment of this problem seems equally effective in this regard. Secondly, as Boethius himself readily saw (and pointed out) the doctrine of God's timelessness entails the denial of the doctrine of divine *fore*knowledge (Ch. 6, sec. III, subsection (*a*)). For Boethius, God is not, to use Augustine's words, 'prescient of all future things'. As Augustine anticipated (see footnote 29 of Ch. IV), this consequence of the Boethian solution to the foreknowledge problem is not in accord with the standard Christian concept of God. That God has prior knowledge of the events and circumstances of the temporal world is a claim that is affirmed in both the Old and New Testaments.[14] It is reaffirmed in a number of important confessional documents of the Christian tradition.[15] Surely this conflict must be counted on the negative side of the ledger when estimating the 'scientific adequacy' of the doctrine of timelessness.

Of course, it may be (as I argued in the second section of Ch. 7) that the conflict between the doctrine of timelessness and the standard Christian view concerning God's know-

The Justification of the Doctrine of Timelessness: Schleiermacher

ledge is even more intense than these reflections on the limited topic of *fore*knowledge would suggest. It may be that the real problem is not whether a timeless individual could have foreknowledge of the future, but whether a timeless individual could have knowledge of anything at all. If, as I suggested, the concept of the timeless knower is ultimately deficient, this would have important negative implications as regards the 'scientific' adequacy of the doctrine of timelessness. That God is a knowledgeable individual is surely to be counted as a central theme in the datum discourse of Christian theology.

(*d*) In technical, theological texts of the Christian tradition, God is usually not described as *a* person – this description is usually reserved for each of the three individual members of the Trinity. Still, for the Christian, features usually qualifying persons (and only persons) are features that are possessed pre-eminently by God. God is described as a loving individual having purposes and plans that are worked out in the development of his creation. God is usually thought of as an individual that can be approached in prayer and who is responsive to the needs and desires of finite beings. However, if God is timeless, it is not at all clear that any of these themes can be retained. Kneale, Coburn and Schleiermacher have urged that a timeless being could not act purposefully – i.e., could have plans (Ch. 7). We have also seen that if God is timeless, He could not be affected or prompted by another nor could He respond to the needs and desires of finite beings. When this set of consequences is put together with the others mentioned in Ch. 7, the conclusion would appear to be that a timeless individual could not be counted as a person – or, even if it could still be counted as a person, a timeless being would not qualify as very much of a person. Again, the doctrine of timelessness seems to be running into serious conceptual conflict with another theme standard in Christian thinking. Even though Christians would agree that God is not *a* person, the real question is whether the category of

God and Timelessness

personality could have *any* application to an individual that is timeless.

(*e*) With 'eternity' understood as 'timeless', the Christian theologian is provided with a ready interpretation of the predicate-terms 'immutable' and 'incorruptible'. Both are to be interpreted in their strongest possible senses. Further, these predicates, when so interpreted, constitute a logical cluster (more or less rigorous) as described in the third chapter of this essay. This cluster also includes the predicate 'ingenerable' and the predicate 'incorporeal'. It would thus appear that as regards this important range of the negative predicates usually used to characterize God, the claim that God is timeless has considerable 'scientific' value. It is not only coherent with, but actually 'points toward' these other elements in the traditional concept of God.

However, it seems to me that there is an important question that must be raised at this point too.

Assume for the moment that if a given individual is timeless, that individual is immutable in the strong sense of 'immutable'. This is probably right. Assume, too, that if a given individual is immutable in the strong sense of 'immutable', that individual is also timeless. This may be right but is much less clear. 'N(x) (If x is God then N(x does not have temporal extension or temporal location)) entails and is entailed by 'N(x) (If x is God then N(x does not change))'. A given theological proposal has 'scientific' value in so far as it coheres with other dogmas of the faith. We could now conclude that the doctrine of timelessness has considerable 'scientific' value if we could show (or assume) that the doctrine of immutability formulated in the second half of the schema just given is a dogma of the Faith. But is it? Christians affirm that God is immutable. This may be intended as a necessary truth. But the above formula says that what is necessarily true is that it is logically impossible for the individual that is God to change in any way whatsoever. It tells us that in order to be God, an individual must be such that he would not be the individual he is if he were

The Justification of the Doctrine of Timelessness: Schleiermacher

to undergo even the slightest change. Is this what the Christian means when he says that God is immutable? The issues that need to be examined here are two in number, *viz.*, (1) when the Christian says that Yahweh cannot change, does he mean that He cannot change *in any way whatsoever*; and (2) when the Christian says that Yahweh cannot change, is the term 'cannot' in 'cannot change' to be understood as expressing *logical* impossibility?

Let me propose an alternative way of understanding the notion of God's immutability.

Schleiermacher said that *infinity* is an attribute of God's *attributes*.[16] It is not a first-level property of God as is, e.g., benevolence. God is infinite in that He is infinitely powerful, infinitely wise, infinitely benevolent, etc. This is to say that each of God's attributes is unlimited or perfect – God possesses what I have called the 'exemplary version' of power, wisdom, benevolence, etc. It seems to me that the term 'immutable' functions in the discourse of religion in something like this same way. I want to propose that when the Christian says that God is immutable, what he means is that God cannot change as regards His power, benevolence, etc. I shall add that on this analysis, the force of 'cannot' in 'cannot change' must be understood differently depending on the specific first-level attribute under consideration. A brief elaboration of this idea follows.

God is perfectly (i.e., infinitely) benevolent. But, further, God's nature or character is such as to provide complete assurance that He will not change in this respect. We say that Jones, having been raised to regard animals as sensitive and precious friends, just *cannot* be cruel to animals. Here, 'cannot' is used to express the idea that Jones is *strongly disposed* to be kind to animals or at least to avoid actions that would be cruel. We have a special locution in English to cover this thought. We sometimes says: 'Jones *cannot bring himself* to be cruel to animals.' Now, God is perfectly benevolent in so far as He behaves in a certain way towards others. I want to suggest that if God is immutable with respect to His perfect benevolence, God's nature or character

God and Timelessness

is such that He cannot bring Himself to behave in a way other than this, i.e., He cannot bring Himself to behave in a way that would make it inappropriate to describe Him as perfectly benevolent. This is the sense in which God *cannot* cease to be perfectly benevolent. Analyses of this same general sort could be applied when dealing with the claim that God is immutable with respect to His perfect justice, mercy, compassion, etc.

However, as it relates to the attributes of power, wisdom, knowledge and intelligence, the notion of God's immutability seems to have a very different content. Here, to say that God is immutable does not seem to be a way of making a comment about God's character. It seems to be a way of saying that God is immune from forces that might damage or diminish His creative or intellectual abilities. If God is immutable with respect to, e.g., power, He cannot cease to be powerful. The 'cannot' in 'cannot cease to be powerful' expresses a *causal* concept. God is such that nothing could cause Him to lose His power.

There are two features of this analysis of 'immutable' that are of special interest in this discussion. First, the analysis makes no use of the concept of *logical* impossibility. The force of 'cannot' in 'cannot change' varies with context, but in each case it expresses *material* rather than logical impossibility. 'God cannot cease to be benevolent' means 'God is strongly disposed (perhaps *irreversibly* disposed) to act with benevolence towards others. 'God cannot cease to be powerful' means 'Nothing could cause God to lose His power'. These are different interpretations of 'cannot', but neither involves the claim that it is logically impossible for God to change. Secondly, this analysis is compatible with the idea that the individual that is God changes in some ways. If God is immutable, He cannot change as regards His perfect power, wisdom, benevolence, etc.; but God might, e.g., change His mind. More importantly, God might be moved or prompted by the prayers of the faithful. To take another example, God is immutable with respect to His omniscience, but the specific content of God's knowledge might change.

The Justification of the Doctrine of Timelessness: Schleiermacher

It might change as the objects and circumstances that are the objects of His knowledge change.

Is this alternative analysis of the predicate 'immutable' correct? I strongly suspect that it is closer to the intentions of the biblical and confessional authors than the analysis of 'immutable' that goes with the doctrine of timelessness. I also suspect that this alternative analysis has closer ties with the notion of a being that is worthy of worship than does the strong analysis discussed at length in Ch. 3. If one knew only that a given individual could not change without losing its identity, I can't see that this would provide reason for thinking that the individual in question is worthy of worship. On the other hand, if one knew of a given individual that it has the kind of character-stability described in my material analysis of 'immutable', that might be taken as a reason for thinking that that individual is deserving of respect and admiration. Also, a being that could respond with love might well be one that is, itself, deserving of love. However, I shall not pursue these points any further. What I should like to conclude is this: before it can be claimed that the doctrine of timelessness has 'scientific' value by virtue of its logical connection with the predicate 'immutable', it must be shown that the *sense* of 'immutable' that connects with 'timeless' can be identified with the sense of 'immutable' intended in the Christian dogma of divine immutability. If there is a discrepancy here, we could no longer claim that the doctrine of timelessness entails and is entailed by the *Christian* claim that God is immutable. A finding of this sort would require a re-evaluation of the 'scientific' value of the doctrine of timelessness.

In the second section of an essay entitled 'Necessary Being',[17] Alvin Plantinga proposes a material rather than a logical interpretation of the modal element in the predicate 'incorruptible'. He argues that the 'cannot' in 'cannot cease to exist' should be understood as expressing a *causal* concept. God is incorruptible in that nothing could cause Him to go out of existence. Of course, Plantinga's analysis of the modal element in the predicate 'incorruptible' immediately suggests a corresponding causal analysis of the modal element in the predicate 'ingenerable'. If this pair of analyses could be established as 'ecclesiastically' adequate, we could no longer claim that the sense of 'incorruptible' and the sense of 'ingenerable' intended in the datum discourse of theology are the senses of these terms that are implied by the doctrine of God's timelessness. Again, the conclusion is the same. There is a good deal more to be done before we can say that the doctrine of timelessness has 'scientific' value by virtue of its intimate logical connection with the negative elements involved in the *Christian* concept of God.

III

I turn now to the question of the 'ecclesiastical' value of the doctrine of timelessness. On this topic I shall offer only two broad observations.

(*a*) In the second article of the expanded Nicene Creed (A.D. 381), it is affirmed that Christ was begotten of the Father 'before the ages (Aeons)'. This formula had occurred earlier in a number of personal confessions (such as those of Lucian, Cycil, Eusbius and Epiphanius), and it also occurred in later ecumenical symbols such as the Creed of Chalcedon and the Athanasian Creed. It appears to be a firm part of the tradition.

What is it to 'exist before the ages'?

As a clue, consider the following passage from *The Longer Catechism of the Eastern Church*. Article 143 begins with the question: 'Why is it said [in the Creed] that He [Christ] was begotten before the worlds?' The answer given in the text reads as follows:[18]

> That none should think there was ever a time when He was not. In other words, by this is expressed that Jesus is the Son of God from everlasting, even as God the Father is from everlasting.

The point seems to be that to 'exist before the ages' is to exist at all moments in time.

The Justification of the Doctrine of Timelessness: Schleiermacher

The most complete explication of the phrase 'before the ages' that I have been able to find occurs in *An Exact Exposition of Orthodox Faith* by St. John of Damascus. St. John is regarded as one of the most important of the early Church Fathers. His writings are usually described as constituting the first of the great summaries of Christian opinion. It would probably be reasonable to suppose that his account of the idea of existing 'before the ages' would be an accurate reflection of the thinking extant in the Church at the writing of the Nicene Symbol.

According to St. John, the past history of the world can be divided into seven 'ages'. The eighth age is yet to come. An 'age' is a unit of time that is measured by the motion of the sun. Concerning the phrase 'before the ages', St. John writes:[19]

> Before the framing of the world, when there was no sun to separate day from night, there was no measurable age, but only an age co-extensive with eternal things after the fashion of some sort of temporal period and interval. In this sense, there is one age in respect to which God is said to be of the ages, and indeed, before the ages, for He made the very ages – since He alone is God without beginning and Himself creator both of the ages and of things that are.

St. John continues the discussion by addressing his attention to the phrase 'age of ages'.

> We also speak of the age of ages, inasmuch as the seven ages of the present world contain many ages, that is to say, generations of men, whereas there is one age containing all ages and which is called the age of ages – both present and future. Furthermore, the expressions 'age-enduring life' and 'age-enduring chastisement' show the eternity of the age to come. For after the resurrection, time will not be numbered by days and nights at all; rather there will be one day without evening, with the Sun of Justice shining brightly upon the just and a deep and endless night reserved for the sinners. How, then, will the time of Origen's millennium be measured?

It seems to me that these passages carry clear implications as regards God's temporal nature. To say that God exists 'before the ages' is to say that God exists at a time before the sun was created and thus before time, itself, could be divided into measurable units. Further, St. John says that in a sense there is only one age (the 'age of ages') in respect to which God is said to be 'of the ages'. The point seems to be that there is one age (the age of ages) which includes all measurable time but which also includes the time before as well as the time after the measurable ages. God exists in this age. On this account, God not only has temporal location (existing before the creation of the sun and thus before measurable ages), but He also has temporal extension – His life is indefinitely extended both forward and backward in time. At the close of the second passage, St. John is obviously speaking of the sense in which we can say that *men* have eternal life. A man survives (in heaven or hell) through the measurable ages after his death and on into the time when time cannot be measured. God's eternity differs from this in that it includes *all* measurable ages as well as the time *before* the measurable ages.

St. John says that there is an age (the age of ages) which is 'co-extensive with eternal things *after the fashion* of some sort of temporal period or intervals'. Why didn't he say that the age of ages *is* a period or interval? I think the answer to this question is as follows: St. John seems to be using the term 'period' and 'interval' to apply only to measurable units of time. While the 'age of ages' includes all measurable units, it extends in both temporal directions beyond such units and thus is not itself a measurable unit. For this reason the 'age of ages' does not qualify as a 'period' or 'interval'. It can be described by these terms only 'after a fashion'.

This last point seems to me to have an important bearing on a line of thinking that is developed by Norman Malcolm in his article 'Anselm's Ontological Arguments'. Malcolm says that 'our ordinary concept of God, (I think he means the concept of God held by the ordinary Christian) is the concept of a being that lacks duration. Malcolm says that the question, 'How long has God existed?' is absurd. He con-

The Justification of the Doctrine of Timelessness: Schleiermacher

cludes that since this question is absurd, it must be that we think of God as lacking temporal extension.[20] The assumption is, of course, that if we were thinking of God as having temporal extension then we would regard the question 'How long has God existed?' as sensible though, perhaps, incapable of being answered on the basis of our limited knowledge. Now, it is not clear to me that the ordinary Christian would agree that the question 'How long has God existed?' is absurd. St. John's answer would probably be, 'Always'. But maybe this is too easy. It must be that Malcolm is assuming that this question would not really be answered unless one had supplied a precise date or period. With this understanding of what would constitute an answer to the question, let us ask St. John: 'How long has God existed?' St. John would reject this question as absurd. But in this case the question would be rejected not because the life of God lacks duration, but because the question presupposes that the life of God can be *dated*, i.e., measured by reference to the motion of the sun. I am inclined to think that nothing of importance about our 'ordinary concept of God' can be concluded from the fact (if it is a fact) that the question: 'How long has God existed?' is absurd. This question would be regarded as absurd if one were thinking of God as lacking duration, but it might also be regarded as absurd if one were thinking of God as existing in the 'age of ages' and thus as extended indefinitely both forward and backward in time.

(*b*) In an effort to provide biblical support for the idea that the life of God lacks duration (which is only half of the doctrine of timelessness), Norman Malcolm cites the following passage from the ninetieth Psalm:[21]

> Before the mountains were brought forth, or even Thou hadst formed the Earth and the World, even from everlasting to everlasting, Thou art God.

Schleiermacher notes that this passage can*not* be taken as

supporting the claim that God lacks duration.[22] I think we can see why. God is here described as existing 'from everlasting to everlasting' – a standard biblical phrase. On the surface, at least, this appears to be the claim that the life of God has unending duration both forwards and backwards in time – precisely what is denied by Boethius, Thomas and Schleiermacher when contrasting the life of God with the life of the universe. Further, God is explicitly characterized in this passage as having existed *before* the mountains were brought forth. To make matters worse, the secondary emphasis in the text is on God as creator of the world – an idea which if taken at face value would also suggest that we think of God as having location in time relative to the beginning of the world. If, as Malcolm says, this passage affirms that the life of God lacks duration, the conclusion would seem to be that God is a momentary being (having temporal location, but no duration) and this, surely, is not the message that the author of this passage meant to communicate. Of course, nothing of importance can be made to turn on a single passage from the Old Testament. However, I think it is instructive to note that this is the biblical passage singled out by Malcolm when attempting to *support* the idea that God is timeless. One must suspect that scriptural passages conveying this idea are not easy to find.[23]

Indeed, this suspicion is correct. In an article on 'Eternity' in the *Encyclopedia Dictionary of the Bible*,[24] Luis Hartman says that as used by biblical writers (both Old and New Testament) the notion of God's eternity is the notion of lengthy or indefinitely extended duration both forwards and backwards in time. Since Hartman does not offer much in the way of a detailed account of this point, I should like now to quote at length from a second scholarly study of the subject. The following is taken from Herman Sasse's article on 'Eternity' in *The Theological Dictionary of the New Testament* (I include only that portion of Sasse's discussion that deals specifically with eternity considered as an attribute of God):[25]

The Justification of the Doctrine of Timelessness: Schleiermacher

2. The Eternity of God

(a) αἰών has the full significance of eternity when it is linked with the concept of God. Apart from the doxologies, this is the case in the description of God as the eternal God. In R. 16:26 we find this in the form ὁ αἰώνιος θεός (→αἰώνιος). The phrase occurs in the LXX:Gn 21:33; Is. 26:4; 40:28; Bar. 4:8, 10, etc., Sus. 42:2; Macc. 1:25; 3 Macc. 6:12; cf. Philo Plant, 8 and 74 and 89 (→ἀΐδιος). We also find ὁ βασιλεὺς τῶν αἰώγων in Tim. 1:17 ...

(b) But how are we to understand the eternity ascribed to God in the term αἰών?

In the older writings of the OT there is a very simple concept of eternity. The being of God reaches back into times past computation. God has always been. Hence He is the God of old, as we are really to construe the אֵל עוֹלָם of Gn. 21:33 (θεὸς αἰώνιος LXX). Again, He always will be. In contrast to men, who are subject to death (Gn. 6:3), He is the living God (e.g. Dt. 5:23: 32:40).

This primitive idea of eternity changes at a later date. In Deutero-Isaiah אֱלֹהֵי עוֹלָם really means θεὸς αἰώνιος (Is. 40:28), עוֹלָם no longer signifying merely the remote past, but unending time or eternity. In addition to the important description of God as אֱלֹהֵי עוֹלָם, which in similar forms is also used outside Judaism for Baasamin as the god of the world and heaven, Deutero-Isaiah also introduces a formula which is of great significance in religious history, namely, 'I am the First and the Last'. This, too, serves to describe the eternity of God (→ΑΩ). As the Creator and Consummator God is the eternal One. His eternal being stretches beyond the time of the world. He is from eternity to eternity (ἀπὸ τοῦ αἰῶνος ἕως τοῦ αἰῶγος Ψ89, 2). Before the world was created, He was (Ψ89:2): and when heaven and earth have vanished, He will be (Ψ101:26 ff., quoted with reference to Christ in Hb. 1:10). Thus the unending eternity of God and the time of the world, which is limited by its creation and conclusion, are contrasted with one another. Eternity is thought of as unending time – for how else can human thought picture it? – and the eternal being of God is represented as pre-existence and post-existence. Yet in later Judaism there are also attempts to make eternity the complete antithesis of time. Thus Slav. En. 65

described the creation of time along with that of the world. 'But when all creation comes to an end... the times will be destroyed, and there will be no more months nor days nor hours; they will be reckoned no more; for the one aeon will begin.' Here eternity is thought of as timelessness, as in Plato.

The NT took over the OT and Jewish view of divine eternity along with the ancient formulae. There was new development, however, to the extent that the statements concerning God's eternity were extended to Christ (cf. HB. 1:10 ff; 13:8; Rev. 1:17 f.; 2:8 ; 22:13). In the NT too, eternity is thought of as the opposite of this cosmic time which is limited by creation and conclusion. Statements concerning the eternal being and action of God are thus expressed in terms of pre- and post- (cf. πρό and ἀπό τῶγ αἰώνωγ, 1 C, 2:7; Col. 1:26; Eph. 3:9; πρὸ κατα-βολῆς κόσμου, Jn. 17:24; Eph. 1:4; 1 Pt. 1:20). To this context there also belongs the doctrine of the pre-existence of Christ.

God is eternal in that His being 'reaches back into times past computation'. Sasse refers to this as the 'primitive idea of eternity' contained in older writings of the Old Testament. This concept then changes. God's eternity is later conceived of as 'unending time' which is not limited by beginning or end. There is only one point in Sasse's discussion that seems to me to be obscure. At the end of the fourth paragraph, Sasse cites a passage from later Hebrew writings in which, so he says, 'eternity is thought of as timelessness, as in Plato'. But look again at the passage cited in the text. It says that there will be an aeon after the creation is destroyed in which time will be no longer *measurable*. Does this suggest that God is a timeless being in the sense intended by Plato? I don't know. As I mentioned at the end of Ch. 1, Plato's remarks on this subject are not totally clear. But let us suppose that God will exist during this non-measurable aeon. Surely the conclusion is not that God lacks duration or temporal position. The conclusion would appear to be the same as it was when dealing with St. John's remarks on the 'age of ages'. If God exists in the 'age of ages', He exists *prior to* and *through* measurable times. He will also exist *after* time itself ceases to be measurable. This seems to me to be precisely the import Sasse assigns to the other texts he mentions above – excluding the older writings of the Old Testament.

IV

Schleiermacher says that God is timeless. He also says that theological doctrines, such as the doctrine of timelessness, are to be judged in accordance with two broad criteria of adequacy, *viz.*, the 'scientific' criterion and the 'ecclesiastical' criterion. But so far as I know, neither Schleiermacher nor any other supporter of the doctrine of timelessness has addressed himself convincingly to the question of whether the doctrine of timelessness is adequate on *either* of the criteria of adequacy with which we have been working. Of course, I cannot claim that the materials we have reviewed in this chapter exhaust the factors that would have to be considered if attempting to reach a final decision on this matter. Still, it seems to me that the observations I have made above ought to be sufficient to at least raise a question. If the doctrine of timelessness is theologically adequate on the criteria of adequacy that we have been discussing, this is not a fact that fits together well with my understanding of the major doctrines of Christian theology, e.g., the doctrine of omnipotence. This is also not a fact that seems to me to be obvious given my (limited) understanding of the datum discourse of theology. My mental posture at this point is one of wonderment. Given the way Schleiermacher evaluates theological doctrines, how did he arrive at the conclusion that God is timeless?

NOTES

[1] *The Christian Faith*, numbered paras. 3–4.
[2] *Ibid.*, numbered paras. 15–16.
[3] *Ibid.*, numbered para. 15, sec. 1; numbered para. 19.
[4] *Ibid.*, numbered para. 19, sec. 1.
[5] *Ibid.*, numbered para. 16, sec. 3; numbered para. 17, sec. 2; numbered para. 18.
[6] *Ibid.*, numbered para. 17; numbered para. 19, sec. 3.

[7] *Ibid.*, numbered para. 27; numbered para. 19, sec. 3.//
[8] *Ibid.*, numbered para. 19, sec. 3.//
[9] *Ibid.*, numbered para. 27 (postscript).//
[10] *God: His Knowability, Essence and Attributes*, adopted and edited by Arthur Preuss; St. Louis, Herder Co., 1941, p. 1.//
[11] *Ibid.*, pp. 8–9.//
[12] *Ibid.*, pp. 9–10.//
[13] New York, Robert Appleton, 1911.//
[14] Dan., ii, 28; Rom., vii, 29; Eph. 1, 4; Acts xv, 18.//
[15] See, for example, *The Formula of Concord*, art. XI, secs. 2–5; *The Longer Catechism of the Eastern Church*, secs. 124–5; *The Westminster Confession*; Ch. 5, secs. 1 and 2.//
[16] *The Christian Faith*, numbered para. 56, sec. 1.//
[17] *Faith and Philosophy*, ed. A. Plantinga; Grand Rapids, Erdman's Pub. Co., 1964.//
[18] This passage taken from *The Creeds of Christendom*, v. II, with historical and critical notes by Philip Schaff; New York, Harper & Brothers, 1877; p. 467.//
[19] *An Exact Exposition of Orthodox Faith*, Bk. II, Ch. 1. These passages translated by Frederic Chase; *St. John of Damascus: Writings*; New York, Fathers of the Church Inc., 1958; p. 204.//
[20] *The Ontological Argument*, ed. by A. Plantinga; New York, Doubleday, 1965; p. 144.//
[21] *Ibid.*, p. 153.//
[22] *The Christian Faith*, numbered para. 52, sec. 2, footnote 5.//
[23] Schleiermacher cites one passage from the New Testament in support of the claim that God is timeless. The passage in question is from Peter II, Ch. 3, verse 8. It reads: 'But beloved, be not ignorant of this one thing, that one day is with the Lord as a thousand years, and a thousand years as one day.' I leave it to the reader to decide the extent to which this passage suggests the idea that God is timeless.//
[24] New York, McGraw-Hill, 1963.//
[25] Edited by Gerhard Kittel, translated and edited by Geoffrey W. Bromiley; Grand Rapids, Erdman's Pub. Co., 1964. I am indebted to Mrs. Marilyn Adams for showing me this article.

A Concluding Comment

When I first set about to investigate the traditional theological doctrine of timelessness, I was reasonably sure that the doctrine would be found to have a number of clearly identifiable theological attractions, as well as a number of clearly identifiable theological shortcomings. I suspected, for example, that the intimate logical connections between the doctrine of timelessness on the one hand, and the doctrines of immutability, incorruptibility and ingenerability on the other hand, would prove to be a source of merit. On the other side, I thought that one of the shortcomings of the doctrine would probably turn up in connection with the traditional doctrine of divine omnipotence. I had intended to write an essay in which both the strength and the weakness of this doctrine would be exposed, analysed and compared.

However, now that I have finished my deliberations on this topic, my opinion is considerably more negative than I had anticipated it would be at the outset. Plato (probably) thought that the things of ultimate value are eternal in the sense of timeless. But Plato was not a Christian – nor can I think of any reason why a Christian should accept Plato's judgement on this matter without careful consideration of how it relates to the broad Christian tradition concerning the nature of God. For the Christian, God is the thing of ultimate value. It is now my suspicion that the doctrine of God's timelessness was introduced into Christian theology because Platonic thought was stylish at the time and because the doctrine appeared to have considerable advantage from the point of view of systematic elegance (Ch. 3 and 4). Once introduced, it took on a life of its own. But consideration of intellectual style cannot justify the substance of a theological doctrine; and it is unlikely that the doctrine of timelessness really has very much to offer in the way of systematic advantage. On this last point, the evidence I have been able to uncover (summarized in sec. II of Ch. 9) seems to pull rather firmly toward the opposite view. Of course, if the doctrine of timelessness could be justified by reference to the basic Christian concept of God (i.e., God as an absolutely perfect being — a being than which no greater can be conceived), or if it could be supported by reference to biblical or confessional materials, then it might have to be retained in theology even if its systematic effect were largely that of chaos. But, again, there appears to be little reason to think that this doctrine is implied by the basic Christian concept of God (Ch. 8), nor have I been able to find any basis for it in biblical literature or in the confessional literature of either the Catholic[1] or Protestant Churches. Again, on this last point, the evidence I have uncovered (summarized in sec. III of Ch. 9) seems to point rather clearly in the other direction.

I shall not conclude that the doctrine of timelessness should not be included in a system of Christian theology. I am aware that the considerations I have brought to bear on this essay would not support a conclusion as strong as this. Instead, I shall close with a question: What reason is there for thinking that the doctrine of God's timelessness should have a place in a system of Christian theology?

NOTES

[1] In Vol. 1, Ch. 1 of *God: His Existence and His Nature* (St. Louis: Herder Co., 1955), pp. 3-4, R. Garrigou-Lagrange affirms that God's eternity is to be understood as excluding duration. He points out, however, that this item is *not* a dogma of the Catholic faith.

Index

Anselm, St., xii, 1, 4; on God's lack of temporal location, 9–10, 15, 100; and divine attributes, 18–19, 34; justification of doctrine of timelessness, 130–65; ontological arguments, 131
Aquinas, St. Thomas. *See* Thomas, St.
Aristotle, 66
attributes, divine, adequacy of statements on, xii; according to St. Thomas, 2–3; God identical with, 19–20
Athanasian Creed, 180
Augustine, St., 1, 4; on God's timelessness, 8, 12, 15, 39, 50; and God's attributes, 19, 20, 34, 39, 46, 50–1; and divine foreknowledge, 50, 62, 63, 72, 73, 74, 76–83, 174

Boethius, 1, 4, 184; and God's location in time, 9, 10, 11, 12, 15; and God's foreknowledge, 53–6, 64, 72–5, 83, 118, 174; on timelessness and temporal facts, 88
Brunner, Emil, 77, 82

Calvin, John, 55, 64
Catholic Encyclopedia, 98, 173
Chalcedon, Creed of, 180
Christian Faith, The (Schleiermacher), 6, 76, 167
Cicero, 63–5, 66–7, 69–70, 72, 83
City of God (Augustine), 19, 73, 77
Clarke, Fr. Norris, 32–3
Coburn, Robert, 88–9, 91, 92–4, 95, 121–5, 128, 175
Concordia Libitrii, 77
Confessions (Augustine), 8, 15, 50
Consolation (Boethius), 9, 11, 15, 53, 54, 55, 56
creation, divine, 97–119
Cycil, 180

De Libero Arbitrio, 76
De Molina, Luis, 77, 82
determinism, divine foreknowledge and, 66, 75–8, 82
divine foreknowledge. *See* foreknowledge
dogmatic theology, Schleiermacher and, 167–72

Epicurus, 66
Epiphanius, 180
essential predication, doctrine of, xii, 17–28
Eusbius, 180
Exact Exposition of Orthodox Faith, An, 181

fatalism, 66
Findlay, J. N., 21–3, 151, 154, 156
foreknowledge, divine, xii; timelessness and, 53–83; Cicero and, 63–5, 66–7, 69–70, 72, 83; Leibniz and, 61–3; St. Augustine and, 63–5; and determinism, 66; Boethius's solution, 72–83
free will, foreknowledge and, 53–83

Gale, Richard, 68, 69, 70, 71, 73
Garrigou-Lagrange, Fr. R., 114–15, 116
God, syntactical status of, 28–33; semantical import of, 28, 33–4, 149
good(ness), as divine predicate, 2–4
Guanilo, 134
Guide to the Perplexed (Maimonides), 26

Hartman, Luis, 184
Hartshorne, Charles, 149, 150, 151, 154, 156, 159–61

Idea of the Holy, 158
immortal, as predicate of God, 47–8

191

immutable, as attribute of God, xii, 40-4, 47, 50, 130, 164, 178-9
incorporeality, of God, 94, 102, 104
incorruptible, as attribute of God, x, xii, 44-6, 47, 50, 179, 189
infinity, 177
ingenerable, as predicate of God, 46-7, 50, 176, 189

John of Damascus, St., 181-3, 186

Kant, Immanuel, 11, 47, 106
Kneale, William, 122, 175
Kretzmann, Norman, 91, 95

Leibniz, G. W., 61-2, 72, 83, 144
Locke, John, 6, 42
Lombard, Peter, 98, 125
Lucian, 180
Luther, Martin, 103, 104

McHugh, J. A., 98, 173
Maimonides, Moses, 26-8
Malcolm, Norman, 131, 134, 138-9, 144, 182-3, 184
Martin, C. B., 26
Matthews, R. W., 113
Mill, J. S., 17, 34, 143
Monologium (Anselm), 9, 132

negative predicates, of God, ix, 1; timelessness and, xi-xii, 39, 51
Nicene Creed, 180

omnipotence, divine, 1; timelessness and, 97-110, 117-18, 130
omniscience, divine, x, 1, 54-61, 65, 67; timelessness and, x, 87-95, 130
Otto, Rudolf, 158, 161

perfectly good, as predicate of God, 1, 3
person, timelessness and the idea of a, 121-9
Phaedo, 49
Plantinga, Alvin, 179
Plato, 15, 49, 186, 189
Pohle, Fr. Joseph, 20, 170-1
positive predicates, characterizing God, 1-5
power, timelessness and, 97-119
predication, essential, doctrine of, xii, 17-28
preservation, divine, 110-18
Prior, Arthur, 65-6, 67, 68-72, 83, 88, 95

proper names, criteria for, 17, 25, 32
Proslogium (Anselm), 4, 9, 130

Rivo, Peter de, 66
Robinson, Bishop James, xi, 1
Ryle, Gilbert, 68, 71

Sasse, Herman, 184-7
Schleiermacher, F., xii, 1, 4; and spacelessness of God, 6-7, 15; and divine foreknowledge, 76, 82; and divine omnipotence, 97-101, 117; and creation, 103-5, 107-10; and divine preservation, 110-13, 114, 117, 118; and a timeless knower, 122; justification of doctrine of God's timelessness, 167-87
Searle, J., 25, 28
simultaneously-whole, definition of eternity, 10
Summa Theologica, 3, 10, 41, 113

theology, dogmatic, 167-72
Thomas Aquinas, St., 1, 2-3, 4, 9, 184; definition of eternity, 10; and God's timelessness, 15; on immutability, 41-2, 164; and determinism, 66; and divine omnipotence, 98; and God's preservation activity, 113, 116; argument for God's existence, 114-15; and the term 'God', 150
Tillich, Paul, 1, 115
Timaeus, 15
Timelessness, and spacelessness, 6-7; as divine predicate, 6-15; logical status of predicate, 17-36; and logical connection with other predicates of God, 39-51, 87-95; and omniscience, x, 87-95; and foreknowledge, 53-83; as it relates to the idea of a person, 121-9; Anselm's justification of doctrine, 130-65; Schleiermacher's justification of, 167-87; scientific adequacy, 172-80, 187; ecclesiastical value of doctrine, 180; and Christian theology, 189-90
Transcendence, contemporary theologians and, x-xi
Trinatate (Augustine), 39, 46

Whitehead, A. N., x
Wieman, H. N., 149-50, 161
Wittgenstein, L., 116
worship, 149-60

www.ingramcontent.com/pod-product-compliance
Lightning Source LLC
Chambersburg PA
CBHW062038220426
43662CB00010B/1551